P9-BYN-746

A Sucky Love Story

BRITTANI LOUISE TAYLOR

Overcoming Unhappily Ever After

A SUCKY
L♥VE
STORY

A POST HILL PRESS BOOK

A Sucky Love Story:
Overcoming Unhappily Ever After
© 2018 by Rex Films LLC
All Rights Reserved

ISBN: 978-1-64293-000-9
ISBN (eBook): 978-1-64293-001-6

Cover design by Cody Corcoran
Interior design and composition by Greg Johnson, Textbook Perfect

Post Hill Press
New York • Nashville
posthillpress.com

Published in the United States of America

To my little dinosaur.
You were worth it.

CONTENTS

Chapter 1

ONLINE DATING

I was lonely. Really, really lonely.

My boyfriend of two months had just broken up with me, and I thought I kind of loved him. Which was huge for me, because I was thirty-one and yet to experience any kind of real love. I know what you're thinking: "Thirty-one, single, never been in love...that's just sad!" I guess you could say that I was a late bloomer.

He was kind of a loser, too. Tall, handsome, but really into vaping and making what he called "art" in Photoshop. I have a type, according to my mom. If they have no job and no car, then they are probably dating me. To top it all off, less than a week after he called it quits, my ex-boyfriend got married to this blonde Russian chick for her green card *because* he had no job and no car.

How did I find this out? Instagram. Thankfully, my work keeps me pretty busy, so I don't have time to obsess as much as I would like about things, but I am prone to mild social media stalking. My favorite button is the refresh button! Can I get a high five?

Don't judge me quite yet. Reserve your judgment until you have heard the whole story that I'm about to tell you. Or read—not "heard"—since technically you are reading this. (Sometimes I ramble.)

Back to my Photoshopping ex. He had to make it look legit for Immigration, so he started posting sexy photos of her with just two words: "My Wife." I went from being heartbroken, to shocked, to disgustedly furious. Of course, I called him out on it! And when I say I "called him out," I mean, I sent him an angry text full of malice and angst and then hit block. Showed him.

I know what you're thinking, and no—this book isn't about the green card my broke ex-boyfriend facilitated for the hot Russian. You are just going to have to keep reading, because trust me, it gets good.

But first, maybe we should backtrack a bit. *Who am I?* Just some girl who happens to be moderately famous. I have the weirdest, coolest job in the world and it involves this website called YouTube. You "might" have heard of it. And if you haven't, how's life under that rock you call home? Kidding.

For over eleven years, I have gotten paid to make online content. I get to sit in my house, come up with crazy ideas, and then put them into motion. Music video parodies, sketches, do-it-yourself projects, blah, blah, blah. I never really commit to one style. Some people are just family bloggers, others do makeup. I get bored easily, so I am always trying to re-invent my wheel.

There is no better feeling than when I have busted my butt on a video, uploaded it, and then get to witness the response from the sea of internet strangers I call family.

Can I tell you a secret? For someone who lives such a public life, I am kind of a loner. I think I just prefer existing behind a computer screen. Socializing with faceless users in the comment sections of my videos. Over a million people have subscribed to my YouTube channel throughout the years, and thousands of uploads later, the relationships that I nurture the most are those with virtual strangers.

Not that I don't have a lot of friends in "real life," but I am always working. Frankly, I love human beings, but I also find them exhausting. I'm a "once every few weeks let's hang out, rarely text, never talk on the phone" kind of a friend. My idea of a fun night is takeout, movies, and going to bed by 10:00 p.m. Cliché? Yes! Netflix and chill FTW!

Rarely, if ever, do I venture to clubs or bars or any kind of social event. This created a problem. To *actually* meet someone of the opposite sex, you have to *actually* leave your house, right? I kept hoping it would just magically happen. Like I would be at Soul Cycle and some hottie with a twelve-pack would just happen to be on the bike next to me.

He wouldn't care that I was tall and skinny with bangs and frizzy long hair. My slim figure in desperate need of a tan. I am really selling myself, huh? Honestly, I am not that bad looking. Big blue eyes and my hair, even though it is frizzy, is thick and long. I like to think the rest of me is like an uncoordinated ballerina. I can't dance, but I look graceful.

Love has almost happened for me a few times, but I blame my past failures on my early pursuit of athletics.

I grew up playing soccer, tennis, and a few other sports, which I think made me overly aggressive. If I want something, I go after it, but that doesn't work with men. It took me turning thirty to realize that the male species enjoys mind games. They like to be the ones to text first, pursue, decide where you go on your first few dates, and eventually, make the first move. I am a feminist at heart, but men are men and women are women. There are base instincts there, and men like to be the hunters. Ugh, boring.

Flash forward to 2015 and I am thirty-one years old. I have a great job, great friends that I never see, an adorable Spanish-style bungalow from the 1920s. I am completely and utterly alone. Sitting in my bathrobe in the living room of my hipster house, surrounded by built-ins full of antiques and knickknacks I have painstakingly collected, I grab my phone and contemplate joining an app called Tinder.

It is actually my friend John's fault. I was in Florida for a convention when he pulled out his phone and proclaimed, "I am gonna find myself a date." At first, I was kind of hurt, because I kind of liked John. Even though he was too short for me and a total man slut, he had gorgeous brown eyes and a face full of freckles. Did I mention he was a yoga instructor on the side? I had seen him without a shirt on...for work, of course. Pretty sure that I was drooling.

Sad to say, but I always inevitably become one of the guys. The one that gets invited to do the guy stuff, because I am too wholesome to date, too soon to marry, and too much fun to be around to actually get around to deciding if they should date or marry me. At least I am smart enough to know that I am easily friend-zoned.

It was not always this way. If you had a penis, I used to be terrified of you. All through high school, I had a crush on this one guy, partially because he was the only male taller than me in the entire school. My teenage infatuation would have paired nicely with my lanky six-foot frame, and it didn't hurt that he was easy on the eyes. We just stared at each other for four years, never actually going on a real date. I like to think that the feelings were mutual, but he was popular and I was a drama nerd with acne. It was purely one-sided.

As I was saying before I went off on a tangent, back in 2015, I was sitting in my living room in my old bathrobe, sick of being the prude-ish friend that you texted out of boredom. If love hadn't found me, I was going to find love. My biological clock wasn't ticking, but I thought it was time that I found something tangible. For example, my parents were married for thirty-eight years before my dad passed away from cancer. Their relationship wasn't perfect, but they were perfect for each other.

I wanted that for myself.

Hello, modern technology! In a matter of minutes, I had a profile on Tinder featuring my "sexy" photos, which for me involved being fully clothed. There was a headshot from that one day when I magically was able to blow-dry my hair perfectly straight. Another photo of me sitting in the car. The sun had hit my locks just right and I looked like a mother f-ing goddess. (I don't use the "F" word very often, it just sounds wrong when I say it.) And finally, a photo of me in a short dress, heels, and red lipstick, standing next to a window looking like something out of the 1950s.

I was satisfied with my work! I had photos—but not too many photos—and my description of myself was short with strategic emojis. Heck, I would date me! My fingers and fate launched me into my love-hate relationship with online dating. I cannot tell you how many times I have deleted Tinder, only to re-install it in a moment of weakness. The app is designed like a slot machine for romantic prospects. You keep hoping that the next swipe, the next photo, will lead you to that genetic jackpot.

But it turns out, most people on the app are just looking for sex. They weren't shy about it, either! I would match with some nice, wholesome looking guy who had a photo of him hugging his mom, only to get a raunchy message moments later! "Hey beautiful, why don't you come over later and put those lips to good use...." Block. Delete. Barf.

This wasn't Tinder's fault, or apps like it. It was just the reality of our society and the hook-up culture which had become the norm. I am sure that even on the most wholesome dating sites, men and women ran into the very same problem.

One of my first in-person dates was with a male model from New York. He. Was. Stunning. Can you call a guy "stunning"? Whatever, you get it, he was yummy. We decided to meet in Griffith Park in Los Angeles for a hike. Exercise and social interaction? Two birds with one stone. Even if I ended up not liking the dude, at least I got a workout in.

Swoon. He was even better looking than his photos. Not trying to be shallow, but attraction for me is always first physical, then mental. From his long wavy blonde hair, crystal blue eyes, bad-boy-looking-for-a-nice-girl vibe. Everything about him was my type. His sweat pants were worn looking by design, and his muscle shirt exposed his chiseled arms—which were hard-earned. I even liked his "mun"—the male version of a bun. Not all guys can pull off a "mun," but he was a "mun" artist.

Mr. Mun explained how he had hit the pause button on modeling and was working for a solar energy company. The guy had a house, a car, a job he was passionate about, and goals. The first hour of the hike was going swimmingly...until he got to the part where we talked about our childhoods. I grew up in a town with 2,500 people. He grew up on a compound with one hundred and fifty. My father was an airline pilot, while his father was the leader of a doomsday cult in Wisconsin. Mr. Mun was also on the NSA watch list, so he wasn't allowed to fly out of the United States because of his cult leader parent, spent the previous year in Hawaii living in a hut smoking peyote, and hated animals.

I hope you are laughing right now, because you can't make this stuff up.

This led to a string of even more awkward dates. I went to church with this one guy who looked nothing like his photos...or maybe he did when they were taken *ten years ago*! The dandruff and the bad breath were what really got me. Another movie date with a dude who literally fell asleep and started snoring in the theatre. Coffee with another handsome fella, but he was clearly not over his ex-girlfriend, who he talked about during the...entire...duration of our time together.

This led me to my Photoshop artist boyfriend! His name was Samuel, and I think I fell first for his amber-colored eyes. They were speckled with green, and strikingly unusual. I didn't fall for his wallet, because the boy was sleeping on his friend's floor and filming/editing videos for some vape shop in Glendale. Sigh. But Samuel had this little boy charm—he was overly enthusiastic about everything and sent me sweet texts from the very beginning. All this made me overlook the fact that he smoked all day long and was clinically depressed.

Maybe I thought I could save him? Or help him to get back on track in life. You know the Wounded Dove Syndrome? I always seemed to pick men that needed me. Our whirlwind romance lasted for two months. For whatever reason, towards the end of our relationship, I thought I kind of loved him.

That was until he called it off. We had ventured one night to Griffith Observatory to look at the stars, laughing and talking with ease. He held my hand, leaning in for a kiss while we watched a film about the observatory's construction. Romantic? Very.

On the car ride home, he started blurting out, "You're too good for me. I can't do this. Brittani, I am messed. I am still in love with my ex." You should have seen my face: pure and total shock. What made it even worse is that he kept changing his mind. One day, he wanted to be together; the next, just friends.

Talk about confusing! That was until I figured out exactly *why* he had broken up with me.

Did he think I wouldn't see the Instagram posts? I mean, we followed each other, his photos popped up in my feed, it wasn't rocket science. Samuel had ended things so he could marry some stranger for money, helping her acquire a green card in the process. That is when I hate-texted, blocked him, and instantly looked for a rebound. Instead of getting a job, he got a wife.

Still bitter? You caught me. Talk about a pity party. I cried for a week, ate a lot of chocolate, worked out continuously so I could continue to eat chocolate, and re-installed Tinder for the last time. I wanted to find someone better than Samuel, someone with goals and ambition. Someone who was a man. It was high time I found someone who had their shit together.

That was when I spotted Milos. I almost swiped left, but fate stopped my hand. His photos were self-involved, but they definitely caught my attention. He was like a Ken doll, but human. Perfect. There was one with him shirtless, sporting only a pair of blue jeans while holding a knife and slicing a grapefruit. It was obviously staged and taken by a professional photographer. Not that it mattered. His golden-blonde hair, blue eyes, and sun-kissed skin more than made up for him knifing the citrus.

Another photo showed Milos on a plane, with his hoodie up, all brooding and mysterious. Yet another one of him laying on a bed of sorts with an adorable English bulldog puppy, which was using his head as a pillow. The last photo showed Milos lounging on a boat with an oar draped across his shoulders. The white tank top only drawing more attention to his bulging biceps.

What did I learn from these four photos? He was hot, rich, and he knew it.

Even his description about himself was subtle, but confident. "6' 2" tennis player and doctor. From Europe."

"Hi Milos, you seem like a total douche," I whispered to myself, but I swiped right anyways. My player meter was in the red, danger, turn-back-now-while-you-still-can zone! But you don't become a doctor without years of hard work and dedication. He couldn't help his affluence any more than I could help my clumsiness. Those dimples, too. I knew it was a dead-end street, but I couldn't help exploring the possibility.

Milos messaged me literally less than a minute after we had "matched."

"Hi Brittani. How are you? You are very beautiful."

Oh, he thinks I am beautiful? Please do continue. I typed back my response and hit send:

"Hi Milos, thank you! Very kind! ;)"

Well shoot, I was intrigued. My phone dinged again. "Can I have your number? I would prefer to text you."

He wasn't wasting any time! Pause. Deep breath. Please don't be a booty call. Please PLEASE don't be a booty call. Could I have possibly, finally found someone decent? I prayed to the Tinder Gods for a miracle. "Sure, why not!"

I don't think I was really ready to date—it had been only two weeks since Samuel—but maybe the universe didn't want me to hurt and brood for months. Maybe it was throwing me a freaking bone for once! I paused, and then gave him my digits and tried to keep myself busy for the next ten minutes by pacing the wood floors in my bedroom, intermittently biting my fingernails. The worst feeling in the world is waiting.

Finally, my phone dinged, and the kind of ding that let me know it was a text. I let out a breath I didn't know I was holding, and lifted my cellphone to my eager face. "Hi, it's Milos."

Yes! I may or may not have danced around the room. I waited another ten minutes before responding with a simple but classy, "Wasssssssup? ;)"

We made small talk. He was in Los Angeles for work, and had resided in California for two years. As excited as I was for the distraction, part of me was holding back. I wasn't ready to get hurt again. He talked; I politely flirted. Milos seemed too special and accomplished to pass up, but I didn't feel like myself.

My wall was up, and it was twenty feet high with spikes, motion-activated lasers, and a moat with radioactive dolphins. Why did I feel like I was cheating on Samuel? My heart still belonged to him, even though he didn't deserve it.

Ding. "Can I text you tomorrow? Would you like that?" Despite myself, I smiled and replied: "If you must! ;)"

He did text me the next day, and the day after that, and the day after that. The next five days straight, my phone would randomly light up. This man was bold enough to know what he wanted and go after it. Or the stalker type. I was hoping for the first!

It was a beautiful Friday in July. The weather was unusually cool. LA is known for its hot summers, but this Friday was a blissful relief. My phone chimed, it was Milos of course. "What are you doing this Sunday? We should meet!"

"We should, should we? What do you suggest?"

"How about coffee, or beach?"

Me? In a bathing suit? I would blind him with my whiteness! "Coffee! Coffee is good!" I didn't actually drink coffee—my demeanor is naturally high-strung and caffeine makes me jumpy. Tea is more my speed, but I didn't need to explain this.

"We can just wing it!"

"Sounds good my dear! Talk tomorrow!"

"My dear"? Hmmm. Kind of soon, but maybe cultural differences?

The prospect of meeting my European mystery doctor might have just put me in the best mood ever. There was pep in my step, a grin on my face, and a tiny flicker burning with possibility. That was until Saturday came and went with cellular silence. Typical. I get my hopes up only to be disappointed.

Why text me for almost a week, and make plans, only to blow me off? Enough. I had had enough of dating. Tinder? Delete. Maybe I was destined to own twenty turtles, grow my own food, and live in the woods. So be it.

I forced myself to forget about the charming, but flaky, foreigner and focus back on my career.

Two weeks later, I was in Anaheim, California for another convention. One of those things where super fans show up to listen to Youtubers like myself talk, sign their posters, and take an exorbitant number of selfies. My internet star status wasn't as huge as some of my peers, but my "fans" were sweet and dedicated! They gave the best hugs and made me feel special. Some of them might even be reading this book right now. If that is the case, hi! I love you!

One of the perks of these conventions is that they usually put you up in a hotel, providing you with a few full-access passes to invite a friend or manager. I chose to bring my friend Lawrence. He was my BFF, gayer than gay, the funniest man I have ever met, and a professional ballroom dancer. He could make even me look good out on the dance floor. Lawrence was the perfect date because he was a constant in my life, and non-threatening because he liked boys, too.

On our second-to-last night, while on our way to sushi with Lawrence's boyfriend, I heard my phone ding. What do you know? It was Milos.

"Hi Brittani! What are you up to?"

11:00 p.m. on a Saturday? He was looking for a hookup.

"In Orange County for work. You?"

"I am in Marina Del Rey with my cousin. Come join us for drinks!"

Have I told you guys yet that I don't drink? I don't drink, and let me tell you why. The first time I did consume alcohol was in college. My suite mates at my dorm had peer-pressured me into drinking six ounces of straight vodka at four o'clock in the afternoon on a weekday.

Oh, it was bad. I regressed to the mental state of a kindergartener. Our hall was shaped like a square, with grass in the middle. Had you been there, you would have witnessed me picking handfuls of grass and throwing it at people, and then running away in sheer terror. I somehow ended up in the nasty communal bathroom in the dorm common area, talking to the toilet about this guy Mac that lived above me. The toilet was a good listener.

This led to me crawling up the stairs, letting myself into Mac's dorm room, which was magically unlocked, and writing him a poem. "I want to go to MacDonald's, and buy a Big Mac, Mac and cheese, bologna is whack!" End poem. I even drew him a picture: myself as a stick figure holding a hamburger. Needless to say, he never talked to me again.

My suite mates finally tired of my antics. They escorted me to the food court where I proceeded to steal someone's churro off their plate, shoving it into my mouth and chewing as if my life depended on it. I also got a taste of what it's going to be like when I enter menopause. Hot flashes lit up my face like a Christmas tree, even hours after I had finally sobered up.

I am not in contact with any of my college friends. I wonder why.

The second time I consumed alcohol was during a really bad week. It was right before finals, my suite mate found out her basketball player boyfriend was cheating on her, and my other suite mate was failing calculus. Many alcoholic beverages and tears flowed that night. Ugh. The next day, a massive headache and self-loathing made me vow to never touch the stuff again.

Milos didn't need to know this about me, and I was mad at him for blowing me off.

"We are going to be here for a while if you want to join?"

"Sorry, working." No smiley face...he didn't deserve it.

Sunday came and went. Drove back to LA, dropping Lawrence off at his house along the way. Honestly, I had forgotten about Milos. He had wasted my time and I was more concerned with unpacking and catching up on the latest episode of *The Bachelor*.

Monday morning, my phone beeps.

"Hello Brittani, what are you doing?"

Should I be honest? Eating potato chips with a face mask on while watching catty women fight over some guy on my laptop.

"Working." One-word answer, all he was going to get from now on.

"Would you like to meet up?"

Okay, he wasn't getting the hint. "Look, to be honest, we had plans and you blew me off. Best of luck!"

Ding. "No, you don't understand, give me another chance, please! What are you doing in forty-five minutes?"

Another moment of fate in my life. I could have sat, with my clay mask and greasy hair, watching my favorite reality show, but I had never before had a guy ask for a second chance.

Maybe he had a good reason for going radio silent and then contacting me two weeks later? My schedule really was open that day, and curiosity got the best of me.

"Why?"

"Meet up with me."

"Now?"

"Yes!"

"Where?"

"Roasters, Hollywood Blvd, forty-five minutes."

Could I get ready in twenty minutes and make it across town in time? If he had to wait for me, he deserved it. Fine. Have it your way.

"Okay, see you soon."

Mask scrubbed off, basic makeup haphazardly applied. My hair was dry shampooed and thankfully still styled from my days at the convention. Only had to fix a few strategic pieces with my curling iron to be on my way!

You should have seen me, madly dashing through my walk-in closet-slash-office. I threw on a tank top that I knew was flattering, and picked out the shortest, yet not slutty, shorts that I owned. Topped it off with my favorite knee-high boots, the ones with the fancy buckles. Ready or not, I went to meet the mysterious doctor who I just couldn't seem to say no to.

But how do you say no to destiny?

Chapter 2

COFFEE

I was nervous. Why was I nervous? Sitting in traffic, running late, my hands were leaving salty pools on my steering wheel. Even with the a/c churning full blast and holding my palms in front of the fully open vents, there was no saving me.

My plan was the following: Show up, be a cold bitch, make him want me, go home, block his number.

I felt like I had something to prove. If not to him, at least to myself. I am desirable. I am worthy. My self-esteem was in the toilet, and all I wanted was someone to look at me with "those eyes." You know, when someone looks at you with wonder, like they can't believe that you are actually real.

If I was an arcade, I wanted to be the gaming console that you won for one hundred thousand tickets. Even if only momentarily, I wanted to feel special.

What was even weirder than the sweaty palms was my mental state. I had anxiety. Not a clinical diagnosis per se, but definite first-date jitters.

Finally, I made it to Roasters, found an open parking meter—which never happens—inserted my credit card, and then hastily got back into my vehicle. In LA you pay for everything. There are no limits to the ways you can spend your money and parking is rarely free. In my many years residing in the City of Angels, I have learned to love valet and always carry cash. Audiobooks as well! They are excellent anti-road rage.

What now? Should I text him that I am here? Sitting in my trendy silver Mini Cooper, I couldn't seem to move. I mean, I had already gotten ready, battled through traffic, found a parking spot. What was the worst thing that could happen? He could just be another Tinder disappointment. Another story to tell my girlfriends on our semi-weekly hikes in Griffith Park. My love life hadn't been successful, but at least it was entertaining.

Okay, now I was angry. I was letting some guy who was a total stranger and probably a flash in the pan get to me. Deep breath, grab purse, open door, close door, lock car, start walking. The metal on my boots clicking with every step, to the annoyance of the pavement.

At least I had confidence knowing that I looked desirable. How did I know this? There is a little game I liked to play called "the gas station test."

It is pretty simple, and it doesn't have to be a gas station. Head into any populated public venue before a date, find humans, walk past, and observe their reactions. Staring, raised eyebrows, double takes, all good signs. Creepy flirtatious comments from the elderly cashier? Go get 'em, tiger!

I looked better than I felt, but I strutted up to the coffee shop with false confidence. Trying to casually spot Milos, my heart was racing. Roasters was littered with tables and all different forms of life. Laptops, laughing, and lattes blanketed the outdoor space. My eyes quickly scanned face after face, until there he was. Sitting on the "made new to look old" bench next to the entrance.

I will never forget what he wore. What he looked like in that moment. Blue faded jeans, a tight white t-shirt, and expensive looking tennis shoes. Milos's eyes locked with mine. They popped open, like he had been sleeping and I had startled him awake. Realizing himself, he hurriedly picked up his wallet and keys next to him on the bench, rose to his feet, and gifted me with an overly friendly grin.

This was bad. This was very, very bad. As I walked closer, I realized that this guy didn't look like his photos. He looked better. On his Tinder pictures, you couldn't spot his adorable freckles. Long, thick eyelashes framed his ocean blue eyes. Perfect teeth, kissable full lips.

His blonde hair had been expertly cut, modern. Through his tight shirt, you could make out the outline of his muscles, which I am sure was on purpose. The boy was wearing size medium when his biceps were SCREAMING for a large.

This man was a doctor? I should get sick more often!

Great, my palms were sweating again. We did that thing that people do in the movies, where they see each other and come to a stop somewhere in the middle of a beautiful wide shot, drawn together like magnets.

"Hello Brittani, it is my pleasure meeting you," he said.

His English needed some work. Who gives a...rhymes with "mitt."

"Milos, right? Nice to meet you!"

Stick to the plan, Brittani! Sit, flirt, reject, leave! Don't look at the dimples. Ignore the veins artistically climbing up his arms. This is a trap!

He motioned for me to follow as he opened the front door, a sexy grin and nod of his head to the right indicating that I should go first. "What a gentleman!" was my response as I breezed past, ogling the most handsome man I had ever seen.

What was to my advantage was: 1) I was emotionally unavailable, and 2) I didn't trust him. Milos was by far the most majestic creature I had ever laid eyes on, but I was still mad at him for toying with me. The instant we got into the coffee shop, I relaxed. Realizing that a guy like him would never be interested in a girl like me. Not that I wasn't attractive, but he was the type of guy that could have literally anyone he wanted.

That realization is when I regained focus. Back to my earlier plan of show up, show off, peace out. We stood side-by-side at the front counter, him ordering a cappuccino, myself a daring cup of raspberry chamomile tea.

"You are even more beautiful than your photos," Milos said, handing the barista his credit card, the compliment somehow more dazzling laced with his thick accent.

Not falling for that one. "This is true," I replied, smirking. Game on.

Even with Roasters being as busy as it was, there were two stools open side by side at the counter. Again, like a film where everything had been staged, waiting just for us.

"Why don't you sit, I will bring the drinks?" he suggested.

"Are you sure they won't be too heavy? I mean, you're obviously out of shape."

It took him a moment to realize that I was joking. His face cracked into a molten grin.

"Keep your cell phone handy just in case, might need you to call a doctor!" he answered.

"I might actually know one. Tall, cocky, owns a dog. I hope you're not allergic?"

I was referencing the English bulldog in his profile photo, taken the first day he brought home his puppy named Lui. In case you needed context as to why what I had just said was funny. And witty. The fact that he was an animal lover made him even more desirable.

Sipping our respective drinks, our words bounced back and forth like a competitive game of ping-pong. He was eating it up and I was enjoying being sassy for once in my life. We sat there in that café for hours, the conversation flowing faster than the caffeine through his veins. Three cappuccinos later and I still had his attention.

"Sorry if I seem tired. I was doing surgery all this morning."

"Really, what kind of surgery?"

"My friend Doctor Bernard needed help with a facelift. I am here a lot for surgeries!"

To be honest, plastic surgery scares me. I would rather have a face full of wrinkles that are mine, than have my skin unnaturally stretched, cut, and stapled like a human canvas. When I look in the mirror, I want to recognize the person looking back.

"If you ever suggest that I need anything done, I will slap you."

It took a second for him to respond, an intensity in his eyes as he very carefully looked me up and down. "Why would I do that? You are gorgeous. You need nothing."

So freaking cheesy, but I bought every word. Milos went on to tell me about his adventures at his main job, working in the ER at Savior Hospital in San Diego. He just happened to match with me on Tinder when he was in Beverly Hills working with

Doctor Bernard. According to Milos, I was his first date since coming to the States.

Should I have been honest about how many dates I had been on from Tinder alone? Nope.

Whenever you get to know someone, you always go through the same cycle of questions. Where are you from? Me, Sedona. Him, Serbia. What was your childhood like? Me, played in the creek all summer and ate pizza. Him, private boarding school in England. How many languages do you speak? Me, two. English and bad English. Him, five. Serbian, English, German, Russian, and Latin.

When it got to the part where we talked about our families, Milos visibly tensed. I didn't need to find out every tiny detail on our first and only rendezvous, so whatever he wanted to divulge was fine by me. He was born in 1988, and from 1991–1999 his country was at war. Yugoslavia broke apart and I didn't fully understand the rest, even as he patiently recounted the facts behind it.

War rarely makes sense.

His family was one of the wealthiest in Europe before the war, and then tragically fell into ruin. Milos described hanging out with a group of his friends, jumping from land mine to land mine just for fun. A dare, because they were set to not explode if the weight was under seventy-five pounds. I played on a swing set in my backyard, while he and his buddies located gun caches.

At night, he would sleep in the hallway because bullets had more walls to travel through that way. Milos lived on powdered milk, canned food, and no electricity or running water until he was five years old. I can't imagine what it must have been like. To live in that kind of fear every day.

To wonder if just walking down the street, a bomb will fall out of the sky, ending your already short existence.

"My grandfather, Misha. He had a hotel. There were lots and lots of refugees on the streets, so his friend, who owned the hotel with him, they decided to let them stay for free, right? So, they come back to the hotel, after...let's say, a few days? And everything is gone. Poof. They had stolen and sold everything. Even the wiring in the walls, it was crazy! My grandfather and his friend, they decide to put booby traps in the hotel, in case any of the refugees come back, right? My grandfather's friend was not smart, and he goes drinking. After much vodka he comes to the hotel, and one of his bombs goes off..."

At this point in the story, I gasped! Please tell me he didn't get hurt. I don't really want to hear the rest of this tale unless it is a happy ending with no missing limbs. You know when people start to tell you awkward tales and you keep repeating in your head, "I don't want to hear this, I don't want to hear this, I don't want to hear this!" Only me?

"He was fine, just a few burns and a hangover."

Phew. It was okay to laugh! Milos had a gift with words, even with his broken English. Weaving them in a way that I could picture clearly in my head what he was trying to convey.

Milos's mom, Zora, was a general in the Serbian army. She parlayed her skills into helping to start multiple businesses with her best friend, Nikola. During the war, they took a loan from some Russian friends and started a furniture company. High-end Italian furniture, which, in turn, they sold to wealthy Russian clients.

Zora thought it best that Milos went to boarding school, where it was safer, so he lived in England for a few years towards the end of the war.

He was also a very gifted athlete. At sixteen, Milos received a tennis scholarship to a local high school next to Boise State in Idaho. He told me how he grew up and trained with Novak Djokovic and was on track to become a tennis superstar...until he tore his ACL while back in Serbia on summer break. He had a break on his break! Talk about a bad break! I will stop using the word "break" now.

"So, how did you make the leap from tennis to medicine?"

Not the first time he had been asked this question. "I did MMA for a bit because I was very angry, then served in the Serbian army for a year. I always wanted to help people, and I like studying, so I focused on the entrance exams. I did well, and then went to medical school."

Over-achiever much? Not that I minded. Most of the guys I had dated so far had little to no ambition. It was weird, in a good way.

Nursing my third cup of non-caffeinated tea, I desperately had to pee, but I wanted to talk to him more than I wanted to empty my bladder. "You said, though, that you still work for your family?"

He explained that Nikola had gathered the profits from the furniture business and invested in land, a water factory, architecture company, a coffee brand, and more. He was an entrepreneur and Milos still helped his father figure with the day-to-day operations. A middle man of sorts, when he wasn't being a hotshot doctor.

It was my turn to talk about my family.

We were middle class. My dad, Robert, was an airline pilot for thirty years until his atrial fibrillation forced him into early retirement. My mother, Barbara, was a flight attendant turned stay-at-home mom. And no, they didn't meet because he was a pilot and she was a stewardess. They connected on a plane when they were both passengers.

It was the '70s. At that point, Mom was straightening her hair and wearing copious amounts of electric blue eyeshadow. She was at the end of a grueling two-week shift and the flight was empty. Tediously, she collected pillows, lifted the arm rests, and planned on sleeping as she had the whole row to herself.

My dad boarded the almost empty airplane, took one look at my mom, and decided he had to sit next to her. She was too tired to say no and too angry to speak in general, so she ignored him for the first half of their trip. Finally, my dad got her talking and asked her out on a date. They were pretty much inseparable after that.

A few months into their love story, my parents were out to dinner and my mom realized she had never asked my dad what he did for a living.

"I'm an airline pilot."

According to my mother, she sighed and guffawed. In total disbelief, she dished out a very serious retort. "That's funny, because I don't date pilots."

"No really, I am a 747 Captain for Northwest."

Thinking it was some sort of joke, my father was forced to grab his uniform from his car and bring it into the restaurant. He had to show it to my mother before she would believe him. Pilots during that time were playboys. Have you seen the movie *Catch Me If You Can*? All the flight attendants were gorgeous, and the aviators were gods.

My mom described how she was weighed every time she checked in. If you were five pounds over your "ideal weight," then you were sent home. Your hair, makeup, and pantyhose were checked. If you didn't fit their physical standards, you didn't fly.

They were supermodels in the sky, with five thousand applicants for every one position.

My dad loved my mom, my mom loved my dad. Their love lasted for over thirty-eight years before his passing.

After I was born, we moved from Minnetonka, Minnesota, to Sedona, Arizona. My older brother was allergic to mosquitos and, in Minnesota, they are the national bird. While gorgeous, Sedona at that time was mostly a retirement community. The red rocks were otherworldly, but the majority of the residents hated children.

In 1985, the lifestyle in Sedona was as follows. One traffic light, no park, one movie theater, one grocery store that was also a drug store, mostly dirt roads, one KFC, no mall, boring, boring, boring. Due to the lack of children my age, I was always approaching any adult in my path.

My mom said I was three years old when I marched up to a woman in the cereal aisle. "Where did you get those shoes?" I demanded, very serious, hand on hip.

Fashionista since birth.

I was also taught to say "please" and "thank you," to have manners. Not yet attending kindergarten, I was Mom's errand buddy. We were at the post office when an older gentleman accidentally dropped his mail in front of us. Being the well-trained toddler that I was, I went to help him pick up the scattered packets of parchment. Whack! He hit me on the head with a magazine. "She is trying to steal my mail!" he shouted.

I'm pretty sure my mother had smoke coming out of her ears.

What I am trying to say is that my family wasn't super wealthy, but they weren't poor either. My childhood was interesting, but nothing compared to what Milos had experienced. The kind of adventures Milos was describing were unimaginable.

Photos on his phone boasted his Tuscan-style development property in Montenegro. Zora and Nikola had purchased the multi-million-dollar piece of land, and so far, only completed half of the proposed villas. Milos also had a high-end flat in Russia acquired from his brief stint in oil, property in Croatia, oh yeah, and a yacht.

"We don't like to take it out that much because fuel is expensive. It was a bargain at nine hundred thousand dollars, but now it just sits there. Why waste five thousand dollars unless it is a special occasion, right?"

"Uh huh. Totally, makes sense."

He continued to talk about lavish vacations his family ventured on each year. Ibiza, the Maldives, so on and so forth. Showing me his timepiece, he boasted about his watch collection, each ticker sporting a price tag of twenty-five thousand dollars or higher. In Serbia, he had a closet full of Tom Ford suits and clothing that he had purchased but never worn. Another photo of his expensive black Audi that Nikola was now driving, just for kicks.

When people start talking about their wealth, I stop listening. Frankly, it makes me uncomfortable. Money is great and all, it makes your life easier, but it doesn't make you happier. The way Milos started throwing around what he owned and how much he had paid for it really started to turn me off. I care more about someone's heart than their bank account.

I think he sensed my shift in mood, because he kept giving me puzzled looks. You could see the wheels turning in his head, trying to figure me out. Heck, I am so complicated I can't figure myself out most of the time! Our date was coming to an end, I was tired, I was over it.

My go-to move when I want to get out of a situation is to blame it on my career.

"Well, it has been awesome meeting you! I have to get going, so much editing to finish before tomorrow."

Poor Milos, he was the nervous one now. I doubt that many women in his life have ever ended the date first. My gut instinct was that Milos was used to girls falling all over him, and I was looking for more than a handsome guy with nice toys. At this point, I was wasting his time and mine.

Uneasy, he started tapping his hand against his leg. "I understand. Can I walk you to your car?"

To be honest, I had had enough of his presence. The boasting and bragging had turned me off faster than a space ship. Or rocket ship. Which is faster? Faster than a space-rocket-modified-car loaded-with-NOS fast. I was done.

As we exited the coffee shop, my long legs propelled me to my car. Milos had no trouble keeping up, his stature an advantage in this situation. I can usually outwalk people, but I had met my match. From the corner of my eye, I saw him shove his hands in his pockets, his head slightly downcast. My mind was set. It had been fun, but he was not the one for me.

After unlocking my car, I turned to give him a hug because I hug everyone. "Thank you again for the tea, safe travels back to San Diego."

"I am actually staying at my grandma's house in Beverly Hills tonight. What are you doing tomorrow?"

Working, because I am always working. "Pre-production for a video, typical week for me."

"Can I take you to lunch?"

This was another first. Never, in all my years of dating, had anyone been so bold. I was used to the three-day rule. Encounter, then don't call or text for three days, lead someone on for a few weeks. Maybe go on a second date. He had honestly caught me off guard, and before I knew it, I was saying, "Sure."

Milos sighed, his body visibly relaxing. That ridiculously adorable smile once again lit up his face.

"Great! Great. We can go wherever you want."

"Text me, I will think about it."

Backing away but still looking at me, the smile changed from innocent to slightly mischievous.

"Thank you for coming to meet me today, Brittani."

I was so confused.

Chapter 3

FALLING IN LOVE

Milos wanted to take me to some fancy steak house in Beverly Hills. Not really my style, and since I was almost positive we were going nowhere, I made him come to me. Fancy usually means tons of spices, small portions, and a ridiculous price tag. But there was no need to try and impress me. I just wanted to get this second date over with.

My suggestion was a funky grocery store five minutes from my house that was also a café. It was jammed Monday through Friday, and well known for its rotating menu of home cooked goodness. When I find a place I like to eat at, I'm like a broken record.

Of course, he sent me a text twenty-five minutes before we were supposed to meet.

"I think I am here. Let me know when you arrive."

Ugh. Sigh. Blah. This may sound crazy, but I was trying to turn him off. Wearing a loose grey t-shirt, old jeans, and sneakers. My hair was back in a pony-tail and the only eye makeup I was rocking was mascara. My outfit was intended to be a boner killer.

Did I leave the house right away? Nope. Return text.

"We said 1:00 p.m. right? I might be a few minutes late."

I plopped back down at my computer and continued answering emails that could have waited. The anxiety started to set in hardcore. Should I cancel? Who cares that he drove over an hour to Pasadena from his rich grandma's house! He should be out doing doctor stuff, right? Drawing blood, saving lives! Not pursuing me.

But I'm a pleaser by nature, and my natural instincts got the best of me. I hate it, but I always tend to put myself in other people's shoes. Empathy? I have it in spades. My brain started picturing Milos, sitting in his car, checking his phone every few minutes while scanning the parking lot. His forehead creased with worry, expecting me to show up at any moment.

That thought got me out of my chair. Fine! I'm going, but I am not staying long.

I pulled into the café parking lot, and of course, he was leaning against his car. Too cool for school. His demeanor was casual, with his cell phone to his right ear. Whoever was on the other line said something amusing, as he broke into laughter. In that same moment, he noticed me.

I received a relaxed "no cares in the world" wave. Not the nervous Milos I had pictured in my head. My eyes did a quick once-over. He was sporting another tight V-neck shirt, this time baby blue. Faded blue jeans and designer sneakers completed his ensemble. The man looked ridiculously handsome and I hated him for it.

Approaching his car, I heard him speaking in what I assumed was Serbian, indicating to whoever was on the phone that he had to go. Putting his cell in his back pocket, he raised his sunglasses to the top of his head, and walked towards me. The smile on his face was warm and inviting.

"Hello Brittani, you look very nice!" he said.

He should have been lying, but his eyes said he wasn't.

"I worked really hard on this outfit. Sporty Spice got nothing on me!"

Milos laughed, not immune to my Spice Girls joke. "I was talking to Nikola; time zones make it tricky and we have a deal for selling our water factory. I haven't been sleeping much."

"Let's get you some cheese for that whine. Come on!"

Dramatically rolling my eyes, I breezed past him. The café was surprisingly empty. Good, I was famished.

I ordered my usual salad, Milos settled on a chicken burrito. The tables in the dining area were rickety, leaning to the side if you didn't place cardboard to varying degrees under the legs. Either the floor was uneven, or the tables were drunk. My date went to set his burrito down, and to his dismay, it almost slid right off.

"Shit!" he exclaimed, grabbing it at the last second. I burst out laughing.

He was used to caviar. Myself? Styrofoam cups and ten-dollar meals. If he was going to hang out with me, this is how I rolled. Still carrying my plate, I headed over to the plastic utensil area and retrieved a stack of napkins. Without saying a word, I indicated that he should hold my veggie goodness.

"Want to see a magic trick?" I mumbled, crouching down and strategically placing the napkins under the gimpy table leg closest to me.

"Ta-da! Let's try this again!"

Milos tenderly set down our meals and waited...success! Relieved, he plopped down into the chair across from me.

"You're good at that," he said.

"I'm good at a lot of things," I retorted, instantly regretting that statement. It sounded slightly sexual, and there was something I hadn't told him yet. Not that I was ashamed, it just wasn't the right time and I didn't want to give him the wrong impression. Might have been the plethora of Jane Austen novels I had consumed as a child, but I wanted an old-fashioned romance. And I was a prude.

Strong morals and unrealistic ideals had put a halt on any make-out session going beyond first base. What I am trying to long-windily say is that...I was a virgin.

A real-life virgin in LA over the age of thirty? I was a freaking unicorn.

Milos was definitely not a virgin. A cheeky grin plastered on his face as he made eating a burrito look seductive. Conversation flowed, Milos talking about a project he had started at UCLA involving stem cells. He had founded a fitness company focused on helping individuals suffering from diabetes. Partnering with a few other doctors, they were designing workout, diet, and nutrition routines to help complement the medicinal side.

"As doctors, we can only do so much. A drug is a drug, but diet, that helps. When you are in shape, it helps a little more," he explained.

It was kind of cute, how passionate he was about his job. Healing the body, not just prescribing meds left and right. No wonder the guy didn't sleep! Between his fitness company, family dealings, driving back and forth to LA, and working part-time in the ER in San Diego....

I noticed the dark circles under his eyes—his only flaw.

We got to talking about previous jobs. I started hustling at a bagel shop when I was twelve. They paid me only five dollars an hour, and I had to be there at 6:00 a.m. every day. I loved it, pocketing a whopping four hundred dollars that summer. My fake nails at the time were a pain, packed with cream cheese and an assortment of gluten. I was a walking health code violation.

After that, I worked as a hostess, food runner, at an ice-cream shop, for a clothing company doing inventory, pet sitter, and at a toy store. Basically, as soon as I could have a job and make my own money, I thirsted for financial independence. One thing my parents taught me how to do was work.

Milos's family employed him when he was a teenager at their coffee company. He and his cousin, Jovan, would load the semi-trucks at night. By the time they were finished, it was dawn. Exhausted and hungry, they would go to a diner close by and order every single breakfast item on the menu, happily spending most of the money they had just earned on food. You know how teenage boys love to eat.

Jovan was still in Serbia and more like a brother to Milos than anything else. Showing me photos of him on his phone, I could see that he was very handsome, but with an intense demeanor. Shaggy dark hair framed a chiseled face with chocolate brown eyes. If all the men in Eastern Europe looked like Milos and Jovan, I was born in the wrong country.

His cousin was now working as a mechanical engineer, and they were still in constant contact, even though Milos had been gone for over two years.

"We are not as close as we used to be. Now we only talk every, what? Two days? Before, every day."

Funny, the cultural differences.

He thought that talking every couple of days was being out of contact. If I reached out to my friends once a month, I thought I was doing good! His mom had coffee with her neighbors every morning, and Nikola saw Milos's godfather, Lave, multiple times a week. They relied on each other, through war and financial crises. Their community was tight-knit, born from desperate circumstance.

When things started turning around for his family financially, Milos had had money to burn. For starters, he opened up a fancy pizza joint right in the heart of Belgrade.

"It was beautiful. Finest Italian furniture from Nikola, right? And we had gelato as well, but this very special kind. Remind me, I will show you. My friends and I loved to eat there! It had the best pizza in all of Belgrade, but I did not manage it well. One of the waiters was stealing the alcohol and the books never balanced. It was more trouble than it was worth, so I let it go."

Night club? He had one of those, too. His business partners ran it into the ground with mismanagement. Milos just wanted to own a bar for shits and giggles. It was still around, but now rented out only for special events. He wanted to sell it, but one of his business partners was in jail for money laundering. Milos's other business partner's father was killed, car bomb. A high-ranking politician with unpopular beliefs.

Apparently, car bombs were a daily occurrence in Serbia. Don't like someone? Just blow them up! Everyone does it! (Those last three sentences were laced with horrified sarcasm.) His birth country was sounding more and more like the Wild West! Fascinating, but bloodthirsty.

Food was consumed and we switched venues, deciding to continue our conversation at the ice-cream shop in the same complex. Milos needed his caffeine fix.

I really had to be going. Like the gentleman that he was, he walked me back to my car. Unlocking my door, I turned to give him a hug, but he started to lean in. His body language was crystal clear.

No! No, no, no! I deflected just in time, his lips tapping my cheek as I somehow twisted and landed in the driver's seat, leaving my perplexed foreigner standing outside. He was surprised, and not in a good way.

"Thanks for lunch, have an awesome rest of your day!" I was overly chipper, hoping to put a bandage on the hole I had just poked into his ego.

"Of course…I will text you?" he asked hesitantly.

He shrugged as I closed my door, buckled my seat belt, and got the heck out of there. I should have wanted to be kissed by my smoking hot doctor, but I still wasn't sure if I even liked him in that way.

Date number three? Another restaurant. I flinched every time he tried to touch me.

Date number four? Eagle Rock coffee shop, my anxiety becoming worse and worse. Why do I keep saying yes to these rendezvous? Stupid, waste of my time. I was the textbook definition of confused.

Date number five, surprise, we went to dinner again. It was like he was amused by how uncomfortable he was making me and this was all some sort of joke. But he was also just so freaking hot. Hated him. Wanted him. Hated that I wanted him.

"If I ask for your hand in marriage, who would I need to get permission from? Your mother?" he inquired, popping a bite of his steak into his mouth.

What an asshole. If I was a cat, my fur would be sticking straight up.

"Too soon buddy, too soon," I hissed.

Seriously, why in the heck did this guy keep insisting on going out with me?

This pattern continued. Him texting me every solid day, trying to see me as much as possible, right up until our seventh date. By this point, I really had had it with whatever game he was playing. Milos picked me up for another round of dinner, on him.

I was in a testing mood.

"Why do you keep wanting to see me?" I asked bluntly.

"Why not? You're cool."

"If we stopped hanging out, would you care?"

Laughing, he ran his right hand through his blonde tresses. "Whatever you want, I don't mind."

"You don't care if we don't hang out anymore?"

"No, whatever you want. We can keep doing this, or just have fun, whatever you like."

The side glance he gave me as he delivered that statement said it all. Emphasis on "fun." Maybe I was sexually repressed, but I wasn't naive. "Having fun" meant friends with benefits. He really had misread me if he thought I was that kind of a girl.

"Take me home, please."

The mood in the car turned ice cold. Heck, I was the Arctic.

"Why? What's wrong?"

"Just do it."

Milos's cute forehead wrinkled, the freckles getting lost in the folds and creases as he tried to deduce why I was having this sudden change in attitude. He made a U-turn, and as luck would have it, we hit every red light. Silence as I brooded. Mentally willing the car to go faster.

"How did I offend you?"

"I am not into just 'having fun.' There is something you don't know about me."

"I am sorry, I do not understand," he proclaimed with total honesty. Could he really be that smart, yet that dense?

"I am a virgin, waiting until marriage. Not looking for a hookup."

Milos. Was. Shocked. His eyes widened, at a total loss for words. Tapping his hand against the steering wheel like a drum, I saw his features start to soften.

"That is actually very good. I admire that."

Great, now I was getting pity eyes. Like I was one of those senile cats at the pound. The one you pet, but their fur—and God knows what else—transfers to your hands, and you immediately try to find soap and water.

It felt like hours before we pulled up to my house. I could not get out of the car fast enough.

"Bye, Milos," I said, slamming the passenger door. I didn't even look back to see his reaction as I fled to the confines of my safe-haven.

Even more embarrassing than being a virgin was talking about my virginity. Probably making you, the reader, uncomfortable too. If you are browsing through this book on a plane, you might be angling the pages so the person next to you can't see what you're reading. I don't blame you.

What do you know? Milos didn't text me that night. He had after every one of our other dates. Always a pleasant "I had a good time" or "can't wait to see you again" message.

Finally, he had gotten the hint.

Morning came and went. I worked out my frustrations with life on a solo hike. My phone was equally quiet, enjoying nature and the absence of my fingers on its screen.

Cooking and I don't mix, but I am excellent at using my debit card. On my way home from my workout, sweaty and surprisingly emotional, I trucked into the closest Whole Foods. As I was loading up my recycled cardboard container at the salad bar, my cell phone dinged.

Three guesses who it was.

"How are you, Brittani?"

I smelled and I was hungry. Besides that? Splendid. But instead I responded, "Good, how are you?"

"Can I see you this evening?"

Actually, I felt kind of bad for my behavior the night before. Whether I liked it or not, Milos was growing on me. Playful, fun, a charismatic optimist who pursued whatever he desired. I just wasn't sure yet if I was attracted to him, or the idea of him.

"I think I can swing something after six-ish?"

We planned, I prepped. High-waisted mom jeans and crop tops were usually my first choice when I want to gussy up, but I do have a few gowns that are flowy and comfortable. It was 7:00 p.m. and I had showered, shaved, blow-dried my hair, put on makeup and a pretty dress. If this was going to be our final, final date, might as well go out in style.

Right on the corner from my house was a juice bar. I found a parking spot in the funky, hipster graffiti-covered lot across the street. Milos was already there, claiming one of the few tables out front. Walking up to him, I noticed that he looked different, tired. Even darker circles ringed his bloodshot eyes, and his coloring was a little more pale than usual. The poor guy looked like he hadn't slept.

When he saw me, he stood up, but his smile was strained. Milos actually looked anxious, smoothing the front of his button-down shirt. His actions were self-conscious. The Milos I had known so far had been cocky, bordering on arrogant. It was unsettling to see him more vulnerable.

"Thank you for meeting me again."

"Yeah, of course, did you already order?"

Great, I felt guilty. My abrupt exit from the car last night probably was responsible for his current state of mind.

"No, shall we?"

He held the door open as we headed inside. I decided on a smoothie, and he stuck to his usual caffeine fix. Conversation was strained. You could tell that he had some things that he wanted to say, his mind as full as his coffee cup.

The breeze felt soothing as we headed back outside with our purchases, sitting down under the awning. Traffic was calming down, but the buzz of the cars on the street forced us to sit closer together if we wanted to converse. Without taking a single sip of his drink, Milos started speaking.

"I don't think that you understand me. Or you misunderstood me. I am very glad that you agreed to come to see me again, because we need to talk."

Huh. Milos was more attractive like this. Real. Humble. In the month prior I had felt like everything had been superficial. Conversations about his affluence and wealth, but no real moments of connection. No instances where we just conversed on a raw, human level.

"Okay, talk."

"I didn't sleep last night. Couldn't sleep. I was trying to figure out what I said to make you change so suddenly," he admitted.

Fine. If he was going to be open about his feelings, I could do the same.

"Well, I asked you before if you would be sad if we never saw each other again, and you didn't seem to care. Then you basically told me that if we just wanted to fool around, you would be cool with that, too. My thinking was, why are we even hanging out? If you just want to 'have fun' it's probably for the best that we just end this."

He didn't interrupt me, but started shaking his head in disagreement. His fire returning.

"No, again, you misunderstand me! I only said that I wouldn't care if we didn't hang out because I didn't know how you felt. I thought you were being nice and were only saying yes to see me because you are so nice. And why did you think that I wanted to 'fool around' as you say?"

"You said we could 'just have fun' if I wanted."

Pause. Laughter erupted as he leaned back against the metal chair, giving it his full weight. Some of his original swagger was returning.

"I meant we could keep hanging out, having fun. Not what you think."

Blushing? Yup, I was blushing. And it was my turn to feel like an idiot.

Directly across from the juice bar was the most amazing donut shop on the planet. They approach donuts like sandwiches, where you could cut them in half and customize the inner toppings. Both Milos and I were craving sugar, so we ventured in and walked out with our sweet treats. Myself, something resembling a PB&J. Milos's choice was chocolate everything.

We took our desserts to the park a block away. It was mostly empty due to the late hour.

Sitting on the ground in front of slides, I really started to open up. I told Milos about my ex-boyfriend and his shotgun marriage. My dad, his cancer, and the total devastation in his passing. It hadn't been the easiest five years for me, and that was probably part of my problem. There had been so much bad, it was hard to accept something or someone that might possibly be good.

He opened up as well. His father, Ivan, met his mother at a hotel when they were in their twenties and they married only two months later. By month three, Zora was pregnant and in love, but she really didn't know Ivan very well. Milos said he looked just like his father, except, according to him, his father was better looking.

Zora thought that Ivan was a professional athlete. This part was true, as he was an Olympic rower, and she was an Olympic runner. Everything seemed fine until she was six months pregnant and they were out for dinner one night.

According to Milos, his father got a call, pulled out a gun, and left without warning. Turns out that Ivan worked for the Serbian equivalent to our C.I.A. Milos's father was basically an assassin.

Zora decided to divorce Ivan. She felt that having Milos's biological father in his life would not only be unsafe, but a horrible influence.

Being the strong woman that she was, Zora raised Milos on her own. His grandfather, Misha, and Nikola helped with what they could. I could see the pain in Milos's eyes when he described growing up without a father. His life wasn't as rosy and perfect as he had first painted it to be.

Sitting in the park, my fingers sticky from the donut glaze, he had finally won me over.

It wasn't his good looks, money, or education that tipped the scales. It was his honesty and his kindness. Milos was attentive, listening to the pains of my past. He was smart, giving good advice, and a word of solace when needed. He was open about his own misfortunes. Finally, he was genuine.

"It is getting late, you want to hang out at my house for a bit?" I asked.

The time on my screen read midnight. Time flies when you're falling in love.

We both stood up, and Milos grabbed our food boxes, discarding them in a trash can towards the entrance. I started pointing out the weird piñatas at the party store, the owner unaware that *Twilight* is no longer current. We made small talk as we strolled.

Shyly, he took my hand, holding it as we headed towards the general direction of our respective cars.

When we arrived at my mode of transportation, he let go with a squeeze.

"I will follow you, yes?"

"Forgot where I live already?"

"I didn't sleep, I may need assistance."

We both laughed, got in our vehicles and made the short drive to my dwelling.

I decided to tease him again, as we walked hand-in-hand to my door.

"You know you aren't going to have any 'fun' tonight, right?"

"With you, I may never have any 'fun.'"

Point Milos. Ask anyone close to me, and the two things I look for in a guy are: 1) Kindness and 2) Humor. Looks come and go, but a sense of humor is forever.

He seemed perfectly at home, sitting next to me on my flea-market sofa in my living room. Our fingers still intertwined as our words did the same. Even though I had realized that I had a very serious crush on him, I love my beauty rest, so I wasn't looking to stay up all night talking.

"You're kind of great and all, but I am kicking you out."

"Why? You don't need sleep."

"No, but you do. Have you looked in a mirror?"

Some blonde stubble was visible as he scratched his chin, contemplating my words.

"I don't need sleep. I just need you."

The look he gave me was intense and hungry. It was the kind of look that makes your stomach churn and gives you goosebumps.

Milos wanted to kiss me, but I knew he wasn't going to make the first move. My "violent jerking like he was diseased" every time he had tried to touch me in the past probably didn't help.

Might as well just put it out there.

"Do you want to kiss me?"

Pause. He smiled, smug and sexy. Taking his left hand, he gently tucked the hair on my face behind my ear. Milos placed his other hand on my waist and drew me in.

Was it a good kiss? Hell, yes. The kind that makes time stop. The kind of kiss where you have to remind yourself to breathe. Milos pulled away first, a goofy grin lighting up his face.

"So, you're my girlfriend, right?"

I am sure my face looked equally ridiculous. A mirror image to his sappy mug.

"Okay."

Chapter 4

MOVING IN

Well, I was screwed. I was totally, head-over-heels, to-the-moon-and-back in love with Milos.

For a while, I thought I was incapable of love. Not the kind of love that you have for a family member or a friend. The romantic kind of love that you can live on. You don't need anything but to drink in that other person, eat up every second you spend in their presence. I was finally living my own love story.

Now I understood the adage, "It was like I had known them my whole life." The only word to describe it was fate. We became so comfortable, so fast. I stopped wearing makeup around him, he mostly dressed in workout clothes. Milos made me feel beautiful, even when my hair was messy and my face was just my face.

August 20, 2015
The exact day that I knew that I loved him. I'm not some sort of savant who is extra gifted at remembering dates, but it was

four days before my birthday. Twenty-four, minus four, equals twenty. I am excellent at math. And exaggeration.

Milos and I met at the end of June, and I resisted him most of July, but by early August, we were officially an item and it was bliss.

He was still living in San Diego at the time and driving up every night he could just to see me. The first few weeks that we were "official," we would grab food, make-out, and talk until dawn. My very sleepy doctor would reluctantly leave, making it back just in time for his shift at the ER. Probably not the safest thing, since I'm not sure if his patients were getting a well-rested, on-his-game medical professional. It might have been selfish, but I was willing to take whatever time I could get.

The more he came and went, the more I felt his absence. I wanted him to stay. Having a long distance significant other was starting to wear on my nerves. My boyfriends in the past had spent the night. It wasn't my favorite thing, usually them trying to pressure me into sex, wanting to cuddle, and being a general pain in the ass when I tried to get them to leave in the morning.

Everything about this relationship was different.

Milos would send me cute selfies during our time apart. Him in his medical scrubs, a typical blue. Sometimes a funny meme about *Game of Thrones*, or an inside joke. Post-workout selfies that I wanted to print out, tape to the outside of my house, and yell "That's my boyfriend!" every time someone walked past.

His communication was constant and reassuring.

Had I found my person? I sure hoped so! He was perfect and he was mine.

We had spent many a night together, but always in our regular clothing. Never getting to the point of sharing the same bed, even for something as innocent as just to snooze.

Lounging in my backyard on one of my many crooked steps, these sentiments consumed me as my head rested on his shoulder, his hand draped on my thigh. Usually we didn't get to see each other until late at night, so this day was unique.

My three large orange trees were loaded, screaming for us to remove some of the fruit weighing down their branches. The rest of the space was a pile of neglected rock and dirt. The back of my house had three tiers. The highest level, while towering over my house, only really gifted you with a view of power lines and pollution. To the right and left were my neighbors, both large, loud Hispanic families that I adored. If you want any kind of land in LA, make sure you are wealthy and have a trust fund to finance the insane property taxes.

I was lucky to have any kind of extra dirt—beyond the actual dwelling structure—to call my own. Even if my neighbors could see in my windows on both sides.

Each year I had saved and financed certain upgrades. A redwood fence and iron gates, year one. Year two, built-in entertainment center in the back bedroom and cubbies in the living room. The backyard still needed work, but the fruit trees came with the house. They were almost dead when I finally was given the keys. My first purchase was a fifty-foot hose at the hardware store.

You should have seen me. It was a Sunday, and I had gone straight from church to my new home. The previous owner had stopped watering the poor creatures a few weeks earlier, and LA was in a severe drought. I took one look at the curling leaves, didn't bother changing, and ruined a pair of cute boots building berms around the trees' parched edges. Saturating their tired and thirsty roots with my new hose. I had saved those trees' lives, and they were grateful. Flourishing with water and sunshine.

We had a fruitful relationship, the trees and I. Pun intended.

Speaking of fruit, there is nothing better than a tree ripened orange. Milos and I had selected a particularly large one and sat consuming the contents, the juice making our fingers sticky. Debating on grabbing another, I looked over at the man beside me.

He had a thing for designer sneakers. They were always brand new and a spectrum of varied colors. Today, he was rocking an all-white pair. His new kicks complemented the grey sweats and a loose, white t-shirt. Looking up, his hair was still wet and messy. Milos had asked if he could take a shower the moment he had arrived, sticky from humidity and the long drive.

I fantasized about what it would be like to shower with him.

Things are getting good now, huh? Keep reading, you perv. Winky face.

"I hate when you leave," I proclaimed, observing his reaction. Being in a semi-long distance relationship was testing my strength. If you know me very well, you also know that I struggle with patience.

"I know, me as well. But you live here, I live there."

True, but it was driving me totally nuts. Something had to be done.

"You should stay the night, actually start getting some sleep before driving back. It makes no sense that you keep coming and going. I want to wake up and you are still here. That is, only if you want, totally up to you. No pressure, it is just a thought."

I intended for that to come out smoother. If this was football, I fumbled. The words exiting my mouth increased with speed until I was practically blurting. My whole body tensed, hoping and dreading his response at the same time.

Milos was with me any spare moment he had, which should have been a pretty good indication about how he felt. But that man wasn't always easy to read. His nonchalant attitude towards life left me confused more often than not. A friend once told me that whoever cared the least, had the most power in the relationship. Milos had all the power and I was helpless to his pull.

You could see him thinking about what I had just proposed. His teeth biting his lower lip, mulling it over. Finally coming to some sort of conclusion, he smirked, one of his many flirtatious little grins.

"You want me to stay the night?"

Trying to make up for my blubbering, I switched to cool, casual Brittani. "You need to get more sleep, why not sleep here?"

When it came to sex, I had made it clear to him that I was waiting until marriage. He knew where I stood on things. I trusted him, what's the harm? That's what I kept telling myself.

"My aunt can take care of Lui. She loves him. If she can, then do you want me to stay tomorrow night?"

His house in San Diego that he was renting was owned by his aunt Mary. Like any dog parent, his main concern was who was going to walk his puppy and feed him when he was away.

"If she doesn't mind, then yeah, you should!"

"You know how I love my pussy."

Milos's nickname for his Bulldog was pussy, which was ironic because he was a boy and his balls were intact. Rolling my eyes at his typical male comment, I tried to wipe my sticky orange juice hands on his face as he pinned my wrists to my sides, kissing me.

It was kind of precious how much he loved his dog and made sure he was taken care of. According to Milos, he had paid a breeder four thousand dollars for Lui. Ridiculous if you asked me. There were perfectly good animals all over LA in shelters that needed adopting. Milos wanted the Louis Vuitton of pets. Not just because of his breed, but the bragging rights that went along with his price tag and pedigree.

If Mary could help out, Milos had agreed to stay the night! My heart was like a pogo stick, jumping up and down with joy. The hottest man I had ever met was my boyfriend, adored me, and our relationship was steadily progressing. Could I get any luckier?

We spent the rest of the evening talking. Milos never failed in having some new story to share about his family, his friends, and his business dealings. He was also a visual person, always pulling out his cellphone or laptop to access a photo that went with his tale. Or searching for a website or article that coincided. We had yet to watch a movie or need anything else to entertain us but our voices. When we were together, it was enough.

Back to August 20. I woke up, two hours' sleep under my belt. The moment my eyelids parted, I just knew. I always asked my Mom, "How do you know when you are in love?" Her response was always, "You just know." I found this answer frustrating, wanting a formula or some sort of instructional manual. But she was right—when you know, you know, and I just knew.

The following morning, I had an early flight to New York. Sometimes I get paid to speak at client events. Brands that want to know more about YouTube and how to properly execute an integration with an "Influencer." "Influencer" sounds better than "Youtuber," so it was often used to describe someone in my field of expertise. Milos was going to finally spend the night and drive me to the airport the next morning.

Most of that day was spent packing and working, the normal chaos that materializes anytime there are pending travel plans. Before I knew it, it was 10:00 p.m. I was still tying up loose ends when my doorbell rang. More like screeched. My doorbell was as ancient as the house. Fashioned like an old school bell, it was as big as it was obnoxious. A silver, round, annoying piece of metal.

When it started clanging, I jumped from my bed and almost dropped my laptop. Startled, but instantly excited. Milos.

Smoothing my perfectly styled hair, I practically ran to my front door. I was breathless, energized, and pulled the brass door handle, swinging it wide to reveal my tall foreigner. His black tank top and basketball shorts, sexy but casual. A gym bag with his overnight stuff, resting on one shoulder.

"Hi," I said, smiling, suddenly nervous.

"Hi."

Milos had an air of intensity. Something was different with him. Swinging his bag from his shoulder, he set it on the floor, closing the door behind him. He turned, pinning me with this look. Predatory. Without speaking, he took the few steps needed to bridge the gap between us. His hands found their way to my hips and he started to kiss me, slowly backing me up against the wall.

I think he knew what was coming before I did. My mind said "slow down, stick to the plan," but my body said, "don't stop, keep going."

His calloused hand went under my shirt and slowly up my back to where my bra was connected, resting against the buckle, but stopping there. The more he didn't try to unstrap my bra, the more I wanted him to.

"Are you thirsty?" Milos asked, backing up. Breaking the moment, acting like the last few minutes didn't just happen.

What a tease! He had me against a wall, kissing me like his life depended on it, and now he wanted water? It instantly made me frustrated and insecure.

"No, I'm good, you go ahead."

Milos made his way into the kitchen, while I stayed put. The familiar sounds of my cabinet opening, him removing a glass, and pouring water from a jug. I quickly checked my hair in a mirror above my fireplace. He returned moments later, cup in hand. His tank top was now off.

My cheeks reddened as he leaned against the kitchen doorway, his top flung casually over his shoulder. This was the first time I had seen him half-naked, in person.

Tanned skin only accentuated the lines of his muscles. Veins wandered over his arms, and crept up from the line of his shorts. He could have been Chris Hemsworth's body double, and that was saying something.

Stunned into gibberish, I made some stupid comment. "Is it too hot in here? I can turn it down."

Milos laughed as he walked towards me, taking a drink from his cup and eyeing me with calculation.

"The temperature is fine," he said. As he approached, my heart started to pound. Stopping inches from me, his eyes pinned me to the wall. With his free hand, his fingers caressed my right elbow, running down my arm to intertwine his hand in mine.

Oh, holy goosebumps.

He pivoted and guided me towards my bedroom. Releasing my fingers in his grasp, he turned off the chandelier light above my bed. My room was still illuminated from the full moon peeking through my curtains.

Milos set down his glass on my antique dresser. Normally I would have made him put down a coaster, because the glass would leave a ring on the old wood. In that moment, my house could have been flooding and I wouldn't have cared.

Whatever Milos focused on, he gave it his full attention—be it a person, a thought, or an action. His focus shifted from the water and was back on me. Closing the gap between us, this kiss was more passionate, more intense. Both of his hands slowly started to raise my shirt, his palms sliding it up my back, once again resting on my bra strap.

This time, he unsnapped it. I didn't stop him.

He continued lifting my blouse, raising my arms as he pulled it over my head, and discarded it on the bare floor, taking my bra with it. I didn't stop him.

Placing my hands on the waistband of his shorts, he guided them down, over his hips, until his shorts slid off.

I didn't stop him.

He was totally and unashamedly naked, kissing my neck as he removed the remaining fabric clinging to my skin. If my house wasn't hot before, it was now.

Now I'm gonna throw some ice on this, and let you guys cool down, because this is not *Fifty Shades of Grey*. I don't want to describe in detail how I lost my virginity because my kids will read this eventually, but I was thirty-two and finally in the "sexually active" club.

Milos was gentle, and experienced, and it was everything that your first time should be.

Lying in bed afterwards, I didn't feel any different. I didn't feel guilty. I only felt at peace, like I had been at war with myself and my beliefs for so long and now I was finally letting go. If God was going to be mad with me, let him be mad. It was worth it.

Milos post-sex was like a lion that had just devoured an antelope, content but still dangerous. His naked body crawling out of bed to grab the sweating water glass still resting on my dresser. My hair was now a crazy mess as I rolled to my side and watched him. Even his butt was a work of art, muscled and tan where it should have been white. The smug son of a bitch stood there slowly downing his ice water, obviously proud of himself.

"You planned this."

I received a cocky smile as he said, "I don't know what you are talking about, Brittani."

Putting the now empty cup back down, he laughed and grabbed his basketball shorts, sliding them back on.

"The water, this, you always get thirsty after sex?"

Laughing, he crawled back into bed, joining me once again under the sheets. It felt natural as I put my head on his chest, his large arms circling me in a protective embrace. He kissed the top of my head as I listened to his heartbeat. Still elevated from what had just transpired. Before I knew it, without thinking, I just said it.

"I love you."

Silence. Milos froze. I didn't dare look up at him, afraid of what his expression would tell me. But I had to say it. If I didn't, I was going to burst.

A long pause before Milos turned my chin, forcing me to look up at him. I avoided making eye-contact. Terrified of what I might see, worried that I had just made a terrible mistake.

"I love you too."

Four words. Four words and my life was forever changed. When I finally glanced into his beautiful blue eyes, they were tender. The look he was giving me confirmed it, chasing all my previous doubts away. I wasn't just some virgin he wanted to conquer. I was someone he loved, and it wasn't just sex, it was more.

Milos fell asleep holding me that night. I found that cuddling while sleeping is highly overrated. Man, was I uncomfortable.

His body was too warm and my bed was too small. But I couldn't bear pushing him away.

Before I knew it, my 6:00 a.m. alarm was blaring, ordering me to get moving and not miss my plane.

We held an easy silence that morning, both of us lost in our own musings. He joined me in the shower, sleepy as he massaged my back, the water running down us and pooling at our feet. Milos made me breakfast, if you could call it that—a few slices of toast on a paper towel as we rushed out to his car.

Heading down the 405 freeway, he was still unusually quiet. The lack of conversation was starting to make me uncomfortable. Was he having doubts about me? Did I not do something right? When he finally had all my clothes off, did he like what he saw? *Spin, spin, spin.* My thoughts were a hamster wheel and I was the hamster.

I think everyone's worst nightmare is that, when they finally "do the deed," whoever they were just intimate with will reject them. Totally exposed, they will see that weird mole on your shoulder, or how your ribs show because of an insane metabolism, and be turned off.

I'll admit, I had spent a fair amount of time on Google beforehand. Researching to see a male perspective on the matter. What was the recurring theme that kept popping up as to what a guy wants when it comes to hooking up? "Be into it, don't be self-conscious. Nothing is sexier than enthusiasm."

Was I just a booty call? Or did we just have a bad connection? Wait, was I about to be hung up on, aka, dumped?

Milos dropped me off at LAX with a quick kiss, a tight smile, and he was off. Great. Finally slept with the guy, and now that he got what he wanted, he was no longer interested. My mom always said, "Why buy the cow when you can get the milk for free?" I was coconut milk, and maybe he was a two-percent kind of guy?

He said he loved me, but words are words and actions speak louder.

Plane. New York. Panel. Taxi. Hotel. Laptop. Write a script. Wait for Milos to text me. Room Service. Check my phone again. More writing. Panic. Start to cry. Rationalize. Stop crying. Hope. No hope.

Around midnight, New York time, Milos finally texted me.

"How was your flight?"

That was it? Not a "I miss you" or "last night was amazing, when are you getting back?" message? Lame. I was pissed, and hurt, and exhausted. Tears ran down my face, burning with shame, which was only making me angrier. My mascara stung when mixed with tears, so he wasn't entirely to blame for my eyeballs being on fire.

This was when the true guilt set in. I had waited for so long for the right guy, the right timing, and for what? To be casually brushed off? I felt like what had happened was a big deal. I gave him something more than sex. I gave him my heart and he was playing games.

"Fine. Thanks," I typed, pain pooling in my chest.

The text bubble with dots lit up my phone screen, indicating that he was replying. He kept typing, stopping, typing again. I expected a long message for the anxious minutes Milos kept me waiting, but all I got in return was, "Have a good night."

One solid thing about me is my pride. If he wanted to be done with me, then be done. It might take some time for me to bounce back from this one, but I would bounce back. I am the kind of person you want to be around during a zombie apocalypse. My will to succeed has always been greater than my fear. I'm a survivor. Cue Destiny's Child.

"You're kidding, right? Whatever, Milos, it was fun, but don't contact me again."

Maybe a tad dramatic...but warranted.

My finger was holding the off switch when my phone rang. It was him, of course, but there was no way I was going to answer. My mind was made up as to what needed to be done. He called again, I sent it to voicemail. Third time wasn't a charm. Again, I let it chime and chime without picking up.

"Why aren't you answering your phone?" he texted.

Okay, so he wasn't getting the message, maybe I should hop on a call? Clear the air, clean break, tell him to go fudge himself. Not a typo, I did actually intend to type the word fudge. Can't stop, won't stop.

The fourth time I answered, wanting to get this over with.

"Hi Milos."

"Hello Brittani, how are you?"

I grabbed my eye makeup remover and put him on speaker, the tears no longer because of him. My smeared mascara was causing serious irritation to my corneas.

"Look, no need to drag this out. You got what you wanted. Now stop calling me, because it is late in New York, and I have an early flight to catch."

He started laughing. His chuckles even more annoying from the echo through the speaker.

"You're laughing? Joke's on you. We're done."

As I went to hit the red "end call" button, I heard him sobering, but his voice was still full of amusement as he spoke. "Come now Brittani, can we talk please? I think you misunderstand. I have had a hard day."

The award for the most perplexing man on the planet goes to Milos! Applause, crown, him wearing a sash that reads "King of Indirectness."

"I'm going to bed, we can talk tomorrow."

He was silent, choosing his next words with care.

"You don't understand me, Brittani. We need to talk when you arrive. Tomorrow is your flight, can I pick you up? Take you out to dinner? There is much we need to discuss. Things have been stressful."

Maybe, just maybe, I was overreacting. My "no longer virgin" status was making me sensitive, and all these new feelings were a lot to process.

"I get in at 10:30 a.m., will text you the info. But I really need to go to sleep, it is 3:00 a.m. here."

"I understand. Goodnight, Brittani."

"Night Milos," I said, relieved and now intrigued. What did he need to tell me?

Great, now I couldn't sleep. My brain kept playing different scenarios, imagining what could be causing him stress. I rolled from one side to the other, trying to get comfortable in my trendy, Manhattan hotel bed. Maybe the drive was getting to be too much? Or we really were breaking up and he wanted to be a gentleman and do it in person?

The one good thing about lack of sleep is that your emotions start to go numb, eventually.

A catatonic version of myself somehow hailed a cab and made it to the airport. Milos had received the info for my flight.

He had texted me some other very generic responses, "See you soon," "Call me when you arrive," but at this point, I really was too tired to make small talk. Thankfully, I finally got a solid five hours of rest on the plane ride back. I woke up to the captain announcing our descent into LA.

A lot of people complain about the zoo that is LAX Airport, but I have always found it comforting. Each person I passed in the busy terminals that day was a reminder of just how vast and diverse the world really is. There are a lot of fish in the sea, and maybe I had just caught myself a shark. Take out the hook, throw him back, try again.

Milos was waiting for me at arrivals, his sleek sports car newly washed. Sauntering around to the curb, he looked sexy and relaxed. What did we have here? A new haircut and dress shoes complemented his dark denim and white collared button-down shirt. In my limited dating experience, when a guy gets his hair cut and washes his car before seeing you, he's interested.

Okay, maybe I had been overreacting.

Greeting me with a smile and a warm hug, but no kiss, he guided me into the passenger seat.

"How was your flight?" he asked, not a care in the world.

"Slept most of the way. You didn't have to pick me up."

Shifting his car into drive, he reached over to hold my hand.

"Don't be crazy, it is my pleasure."

Hot, cold, hot, cold, this guy was worse than the faucet in my first Hollywood apartment.

"Can you take me home? I have a lot to catch up on."

Driving from the airport to my house, depending on the state of the freeways, could take anywhere from thirty minutes to two hours. We got lucky by some miracle and breezed right through. Pulling into my driveway in under an hour? Heavenly. How was the car ride? Awkward.

"Are you hungry?" he asked, sitting down next to me on my vintage couch, like we always did.

"Maybe in a bit? I might have had too many bags of peanuts on the plane."

He laughed, hugging me to his chest, his hands starting to massage my scalp. I was practically purring as his strong fingers eased out any tension I had been holding.

"Did you know that I had a plane ticket home when I first met you?" he said, quiet, tentative.

News to me.

"No, I didn't."

"The moment you walked up to the coffee shop, it was only you. I loved you from the moment I saw you."

Wow, his English was improving, and great, now I wanted to cry. That was by far the most romantic thing anyone had ever said to me. "Thank you," was all I could mutter, my lower lip trembling. So many feels.

"I had a ticket to go back to Serbia, but then there was you. So, I changed my ticket to a few weeks later. You probably thought I was crazy, wanting to see you every day, but there was no time to waste and I had to be sure. My mother's business partner, my family, was counting on me returning. Nikola and Zora need me in Serbia to help run everything. Without me, things fall apart."

I didn't talk, I just hugged him and listened.

"Brittani, I have decided to stay. I love you, I had to be sure you loved me too. After what happened, you know, a few nights ago, there is no way I could leave now. But Nikola and my mom are very, very angry. They don't understand why I am throwing everything away for some girl. I know how incredible you are, but they just don't understand. My family has been sending me thirty-five thousand dollars a month while I have been here, but that is done now. I chose you, so they are cutting me off."

This was where I could step in and help.

My family had been well-off until my dad was forced into early retirement because of a serious heart condition, atrial fibrillation. Overnight, his salary was cut in half. There were no more weekend trips, family vacations, or extra spending money. Groceries, school, and life essentials, that was it. I watched my parents refinance their house, max out every credit card, and work every odd job they could to keep us from totally drowning in debt.

My father got his real estate license, securities license, and started selling timeshares while Mom learned how to use the computer and sold anything that wasn't nailed down on eBay.

I knew what it was to have money, not have money, and then have money again. It was a blessing in disguise, because it taught me how to be smart with my purchases.

"I am so sorry, but we will get through this. Your family will come around, but in the meantime, I can help you. What are your monthly expenses?"

The corners of his eyes crinkled, his earlier façade crumbling, and the true amount of pressure he was under started to show. Disappointing his family added even more strain, beyond financial.

"I have the apartment in Beverly Hills, but that is pre-paid in advance for the next six months. My other apartment in Marina Del Rey, the lease on my car. San Diego, I have my house there that I am renting from my aunt. Those are the main things."

The guy had three different places to live? No wonder he was burning through cash.

"You need to let two out of the three places go. Your place in Beverly Hills, do you think you can get any of the money back?"

His grin was decidedly bitter as he said, "I can try, but the man that owns it only leased it to me because I pre-paid. You see, I am a foreigner, with no credit. People like to take full advantage when you have no credit."

Before, Milos had mentioned his grandmother in the Hollywood Hills. It would make more sense for him to just crash at her place when he was in town, and ditch Beverly Hills and Marina Del Rey. San Diego should be his main residence, because it was minutes to his work. As much as I wanted him close, I cared more about what was best for him.

The rest of the night was spent consoling and brainstorming. It was an awful feeling, even though it was out of my control, that I might have possibly caused a divide between Milos and his family. They wanted him to be their golden boy, closing deals and stirring up more work with his good looks and natural charm.

He wanted to be a doctor, wanted his medicine and he didn't want their legacy, he craved his own.

Whatever storm his defiance was going to bring, we were going to weather it together.

Because he was worth it.

Chapter 5

LUI

know, I know, my last chapter was titled "Moving In" and Milos didn't move into my house quite yet, but it was getting long-winded and my solution was to start a new chapter. This is my first book, so I am new to this whole "tell your life story" thing. Imagine holding a pair of scissors as you cut me some slack.

Those were the events that did lead to his stuff inter-mingling with mine. I have mentioned his dog, Lui, a little bit in the previous pages, but I don't think I have stressed enough how much he "loved his pussy."

That dog was like his child. Every third photo in his camera roll was of him. My text messages from Milos always included a daily Lui photo or video. They were a package deal, and I was okay with it. I have always loved animals, growing up with a ton of pets, so it felt almost weird to be in Los Angeles and not have some living creature invading my space.

Milos was becoming a regular at my house and in my bed, but he was still having the long drive to San Diego to see his pussy, so I came up with a pussy plan.

Step one of plan, invite Lui to live with me.

Step two of plan, invite Milos to live with me.

Step three of plan, get married, have children, grow fat and old together.

I had to be careful and hide the true motives of steps one and two, with the hope that step three was also where Milos saw our relationship headed. Just because I was ready for him to "put a ring on it" didn't mean he was ready to spend a small fortune on metal and compressed carbon.

On one of my typical, extremely strenuous hikes, I decided to put "Operation Pussy" into action! I am now going to stop using the word "pussy" because you are either laughing or annoyed. I tend to have that effect on people.

"Hey love, how are you and Lui today?" I typed into my phone screen. Send. Wait.

Of course, he instantly replied with a cute photo of the dynamic duo. Milos, his arm around Lui's head, who I swear was smiling as big as his owner.

"Handsome boy! I want a dog!"

"You have a dog, what is mine is also yours!"

"In that case, I have an idea."

Here goes nothing. Why was I flustered? I was asking his dog to move in. With the obvious intention of getting him to move in, but still.

"What if we tried Lui staying with me? You wouldn't have to keep leaving him at your aunt's house. You wouldn't have to keep driving all the time just to take care of him, only when you need to for work...thoughts?"

Instantly, he was typing. Wasting no time in his response.

"You want to try?"

Yes! I dropped my backpack and started dancing, fist pumping the air! If another hiker had come upon me in that moment, it probably would have looked like I was getting attacked by some sort of insect.

My phone dinged again.

"When do you want me to bring him?"

We arranged for his puppy to switch houses that coming Saturday. Work was busy for me that week, so it would give me the weekend to really be able to get him settled into his new surroundings.

Hello PetSmart! Expensive, no grain, meat-only food? Check! Dog bed, bowls, toys. I went out and bought everything that I was going to need and more. Have to say, I am kind of the best roommate ever. Two-legged or four, you want to live with me.

All over my social media, I hinted at "getting a pet." Milos and I had been officially an item for over four months, but I had been keeping our relationship secret. You see, I had involved my YouTube audience in two of my past relationships, and the experiences had left me wary.

The problem is that internet strangers get attached. Viewers only get to see glimpses into your lives as a couple and your daily interactions. The content creator is controlling the narrative.

Going to a party together, kissing, sweet moments, edited together with appropriate music. The audience is unaware of the fighting behind the scenes. That is, if you are smart enough to not let them in. And when you break up, all hell breaks loose. Like a dam that has failed, in comes a flood of tweets, harsh comments, and the general confusion that comes with a normal breakup...times a thousand.

Been there, done that, twice. Learned my lesson. Twice.

Therefore, it was too hard to explain to my subscribers, "Hey guys, been dating a hot doctor for months, he has a dog, the dog isn't mine just staying with me. K, bye!"

It was a lot easier just to say, "I'm getting a dog!"

Saturday had arrived, and Milos gave me a buzz, letting me know that they had as well. I rushed outside to meet my new stepson. Even with the car doors closed, I heard a loud panting rumbling from behind the tinted windows. Milos exited and ran around, giving me a hug and a quick kiss before throwing open the back end.

There was Lui. The cutest and fattest English Bulldog I had ever seen. He was mostly white, with a smattering of black spots. A giant pink tongue dipped in and out as he panted away. Lui was like a Disney cartoon character that needed to join Weight Watchers. Adorable, but one too many bagels in the morning.

"Lui, come! Get out!"

Milos tugged on Lui's body harness, attached to a Batman leash. He swore that Lui loved Batman...again, he thought Lui was human.

It took quite a bit more tugging before Milos gave up and lifted him out of the car, struggling with his weight as he plopped him on the ground.

"What have you been feeding this beast?" I asked, more teasing than scolding.

"Everything! I can't resist my little boy! Look at those eyes. How do you resist those eyes?"

Milos baby-talked to his seventy-five-pound animal as I watched with amusement. He would be a good father someday. Trusting me with his most prized possession, Milos handed me the leash, encouraging me to take Lui into the house as he grabbed a few old tennis balls—Lui's favorite—from the backseat.

Struggling up the steps, I got Lui into the house and took off his harness, willing him to explore his new domain. What did he do? Lay down, exhausted by the twenty feet from the tires to my floors.

In came Milos, attempting to get Lui to play fetch. Not budging, he kept his wrinkled, adorable face laying on the ground as he lazily tried to grab the tennis balls with his mouth, only when they rolled close enough so that it would take minimal effort. Lui was only two years old and acting like he was on his last legs.

"Sorry, little guy, your new mom is putting you on a diet!"

Milos feigned being offended. "Do not listen to her!"

It was good to see him smiling.

Only a few nights earlier, Milos was over and took a call from Nikola. He went so far as to step outside to shield me from its severity. Even through my paned windows, I could hear his honorary relative yelling through the speaker in muffled Serbian. Milos, silent, taking the verbal onslaught and trying to gently reason with him.

Zora wasn't speaking to Milos in general; their last phone call had been weeks prior.

It wasn't my choice that Milos stayed in the United States to date me, it was his, but I felt responsible for his current strife. I even suggested that he go home for a while, smooth things out, and make sure this is what he really wanted. He vehemently refused. Another stupid saying was stuck in my mind: "If you love someone, set them free." I was willing to set him free, even if it meant my heart forever being trapped under his spell.

I did my best to support him. My repeated advice to Milos was, "Love them anyways, respect them, they will come around. But it is your life."

His stress wasn't just coming from his family, but also from work.

Milos had quit his job at the ER in San Diego for a potentially better opportunity in Orange County. His friend, Doctor Lancaster, was the head of the surgery department at FHH Medical Center in Irvine and wanted Milos to start working in his laboratory. This would pretty much guarantee him a general surgery residency. All he had to do was finish his medical board exams by December, and he could start his position in January! A huge financial relief for Milos because, even as a resident, he would be earning a solid living.

And the hospital was only forty-five minutes from his current house in San Diego, and even better, it was roughly the same distance from mine. Compared to a two-and-a-half-hour drive, that was an improvement.

Lui and I were kissed and then ditched, while our favorite person headed to meet with Doctor Lancaster, aka Joe. They were going to have a boys' lunch with other doctors from the hospital. The best networking is to just make friends. People like to work with who they know, so I encouraged him to go and mingle his little MD heart out!

My normally quiet house was suddenly filled by Lui's wheezing. English Bulldogs have a hard time breathing in general, and his weight wasn't helping. I had some editing that I needed to finish on a video, so I left Lui within my sight in the dining room area and headed into my office. As I was plodding away, what do you know, Lui lazily got up and brought me his tennis ball. A slow and steady waddle proceeded until he reached my desk.

Dropping it, panting away, his eyes said, "Well, throw it already."

I obliged, tossing it less than ten feet back into the dining area. He turned, waddled, wheezed, picked it up, waddled back, dropped it. We played fetch for the next few hours, with many breaks in between. I didn't get much accomplished, but it was a pleasant distraction.

My phone dinged and dinged, his worried pet father checking on how things were progressing. I assured Milos that his "girls" were getting along just fine without him. An ongoing joke, as Lui was anything but female.

That night, Milos came back from his meeting and stayed over. When he arrived, Lui was already tucked in. Snoring on his new bed in my kitchen, completely worn out from his slow-paced exertion.

My boyfriend usually had trouble sleeping. Tension surrounding his life and life decisions overwhelming him when the day turned to darkness. But with Lui in my home, and seeing him settled in and happy, it was like Milos had finally found some peace.

Little did I know that I got both step one and step two of my plan in one fell swoop. Now that Lui was a permanent fixture, Milos started staying over every night after that. More and more of his clothes were accumulating at my house, to the point that I gave him a few shelves in my closet. We didn't discuss Milos moving in, it just happened.

But that didn't mean that we got to see each other more; if anything, it was less. He had cut his monthly costs dramatically, but he still had bills to pay. His sport academy wasn't doing as well as he had hoped because a few of the tennis pros working under him kept under-reporting their income. That and flaking out, to the point where Milos was now teaching two to three tennis lessons a day.

The lease was up on his fancy black Lexus, so he had to turn it back in. His cousin, Lazar, gave him a ride back from the dealership. He was twenty years his senior and liked to think he was still Milos's age. Tall, like Milos, with straight brown shoulder-length hair, but they honestly looked nothing alike. Lazar worshipped the sun, his skin leathery with age spots. Where Milos's teeth were white and straight, Lazar's were yellowing and jagged. Maybe the eyes? Lazar's were a darker blue, so even that was a stretch.

Lazar lived in Venice Beach. He was also extremely successful, owning the franchise to multiple fast food restaurants. The red Porsche in my driveway was a testament to his accomplishments.

If I'm being real, I found his cousin kind of slimy. The first thing he said when we met was a very suggestive, "Do you have any friends that look like you?" I giggled and responded, "My mom is available?"

Turning pink with embarrassment, Lazar tried to laugh it off as Milos doubled over in hysterics. Pretty sure Lazar wasn't a fan of me from that day on.

Not that I cared. That man liked to text Milos naked photos of his conquests on a regular basis. The women were almost always asleep, probably unaware of Lazar's little voyeuristic habit.

Gross.

At this point, Milos had 2,500 dollars left in his bank account. We car shopped, settling on an older BMW X5, but to avoid him having to pay 12 percent interest on his purchase (due to the fact that he literally had no credit), I took out the loan in my name. The payments were under four hundred dollars a month, a threshold that, with Milos's current monetary struggles, he could handle.

Until his residency kicked in, he had to keep teaching tennis. When he would come home each night, he was exhausted. Starving, sunburnt, and stiff from the physical exertion and long hours of driving between courts. With what little energy Milos had left, he would try to study from his medical books, but he found it harder and harder to focus.

But he wasn't too exhausted to take full advantage of me at least once a day, which I had no problems with.

My world continued on, and work for me was booming! Any spare moment I had, while Milos was away, I played with Lui. By that point, I think I was even more attached to Lui than Milos was. And my big puppy had dropped a whopping twenty pounds since his arrival! I almost regretted it, because less weight meant more energy, and he was a teenager in dog years.

Milos had never disciplined Lui, he didn't have the heart to, and the result was an energetic bowling ball. Racing around my house and scratching up the wood surface.

If I was attached to my antiques before, I had to learn to let go as Lui slowly but surely put his mark on everything. And I mean, *everything*. Nothing was safe from his muzzle.

This should have been the honeymoon phase of our relationship, but our happiness was strained. Everyone reaches their breaking point, and Milos finally reached his. November 2015 wasn't a good month.

Older, rich women gravitated towards his pull and threw Benjamins at him daily in exchange for help with their forehand, or just an ear to listen as they complained about their husbands. Milos was qualified, being a former tennis pro himself, but he was a better player than teacher.

One of his clients, Aubrey, was a concert violinist, owned an island, and was newly divorced. For her, their lessons were more therapy than anything else. Another of his regulars was named Tina. Fifties, blonde, petite, pretty, and the head of marketing at a major online retailer. She had money to burn and a passion for tennis, almost to the point of obsession.

Regularly, Tina would text Milos about what shoes to buy, questions about stringing her racquets, and commentary on professional matches on television.

Did all of these women have a crush on my boyfriend? Yes. Were they paying 150 dollars an hour just to stare at him? Probably. He was surrounded by cougars, and frankly, I found it hysterical. Some bought him gift cards to the movies, others tried to get him to go to charity galas or accompany them as their "coach" to their matches out of state.

Money is money, and he was doing an honest service. If he needed to be a male stripper at that point to make ends meet, so be it. As long as the only thing he was hitting was Prince and Wilson, I was okay with it. (Those are tennis ball brands just in case you're like...what?!?)

By the end of November, after weeks of lessons, driving, and kissing up to his clients, Milos had reached his limit. When he came home after one particularly long day, I could feel his frustration. I was attempting to cook in the kitchen, something that happens only on rare occasions. At least once a year, I get inspired and decide that I am going to start making all my own food, but it never lasts.

What was I whipping up? A dish that involved sweet potatoes, obviously. Maybe I am lacking in some vitamin or another because I am willing to eat anything that contains that particular vegetable. In walked Milos and I could just tell that he was about to blow.

"Do you know how long I was driving on the 405 freeway? For three hours. Three, fucking, hours. And another two hours to get there," he complained.

Tina lived in Manhattan Beach, which was not an easy drive, especially when the requested lesson was during rush hour.

Still wearing his sweaty tennis clothes and hat, he ripped off his cap and threw it on the ground, releasing his salty, spiked hair.

"Do you know the amount of money that I used to make from *one* meeting? Hundreds of thousands, millions, and now I am teaching fucking tennis lessons. I teach fucking tennis."

Don't cry, don't cry, shit, crying. Tears started to leak from my eyes, but Milos wasn't done.

"What happened to my life? Huh? I met you, and now I am here. I used to fly to a different country every day. I could buy whatever I wanted! I had everything when I met you, and now, I have nothing. I had everything!"

It is crazy how much words can hurt. The right pairing combined into a sentence can cut into your soul and leave you feeling destitute. He had chosen to stay, chosen to give up his family's money, and chosen me. If he was questioning his choices, there was nothing I could do.

Words failed as I put down the knife I was using to chop vegetables and walked to my bedroom. I didn't look at him. He had already said more than I wanted to hear. All I wanted to do was crawl into bed and hide. Milos hadn't seen me cry before, and I felt ashamed by my emotions.

Maybe he felt like he owed it to me to stay, because he erased my virgin status.

He was honorable, and miserable, and I blamed myself.

Milos didn't come to me right away. I was almost asleep, my pillow wet with my quiet tears as I heard my old maple floors creaking. Quiet footsteps approached. Lui was snoring on the floor next to my box spring, trying to offer what comfort he could.

I felt him crawl into bed and smelled his deodorant. His head resting next to mine, hair wet from a shower. Milos wrapped his strong arms around me and sighed.

"I'm sorry," he whispered.

A sob I had been holding in broke free. He held me as I cried myself to sleep.

Morning brought a new and improved Milos. Maybe his evening outburst had released some of the pain he had been holding in, because he apologized and kept apologizing.

"I'm sorry, I love you. I was just so tired and angry, you know? It has been a lot."

Of course, I forgave him. He grew up with wealth and privilege and was adjusting.

"You can go back to Serbia, I won't stop you. If you would be happier, go!" I said.

Back in his tennis clothes, heading to yet another lesson, he grabbed me in a hug and dipped me, soundly planting a kiss on my mouth before placing me back upright.

"You crazy woman, I chose you. See you tonight?"

I couldn't help but smile, seeing him chipper again. "If you're lucky! Go, tell Tina I say hello!"

The first fight in any relationship is the hardest. Everyone is on their best behavior in the beginning, and with time, you get to learn the good and bad that comes with that person. Things I had learned about Milos so far was that he was an amazing cook, but he was messy and couldn't fold a towel to save his life. If I carried anything heavy without asking him, he was mortally offended, and he had a secret passion for Legos.

He treasured his friendships, and rarely said a bad word about those close to him. The latest discovery was his temper, but I blamed it on testosterone.

My mom always offered this example when it came to men and I found it hilarious.

"If men are at war, and someone tells them to charge up a hill where they know their enemy is waiting, they scream and yell and run and start shooting. If a bunch of women were asked to do the same thing, they would ask 'Why, isn't that dangerous? Shouldn't we find out where the enemy is first? Is this the best plan?' Men act and think later."

Makes sense, as most males are hardwired in their DNA to be the warriors, the protectors. Women are the nurturers. It is a miracle that any relationships last at all.

We had a few peaceful, boring weeks in early December. Milos had started his internship at Doctor Lancaster's lab and he had renewed energy when it came to studying for his boards. Our courtship was back on track, loving, and supportive. Not perfect, but we were still getting to know each other and calmly tackling any issues that popped up.

You know how I mentioned before that I only saw my friends once a month? Now with Lui and Milos in my life, it felt like even less than that. I kept wanting Milos to meet Lawrence, my crazy bestie, but he was always studying or working. It didn't seem fair to put pressure on him even though I was antsy for all of us to hang out.

There was also one other very close friend of mine, Maya. She was a ravishing black woman who should have been a comedian, but she parlayed her talents into real estate. Maya also happened to be my real estate agent, who spent six months in the car with me looking until we found my current home, and in the process quickly became one of my favorite people on the planet.

One thing that Milos struggled with was English. His brain had to work overtime, translating and responding. It was a blessed relief when he could be around anyone who spoke Serbian and understood his culture. Still, I wanted to show off Milos to my inner circle, but he was understandably slammed. Any free time he had was spent with Lui and I, or with Lazar and Jurica.

Lazar you know about—his sleazy cousin—but I haven't told you yet about Jurica! Jurica was godfather to Lazar's two sons and also Serbian. Like most of Milos's friends, he was also extremely successful. Immigrating to the U.S. in the '80s, Jurica was a killer criminal defense lawyer. Milos liked to joke that "Serbians have their ways" when it came to getting what they wanted. I didn't want to know what methods Jurica was using to be so dedicated to his job, but I had a hunch it wasn't moral or legal.

How did I feel about Jurica? For some reason, I really liked him. He was tall, dark, and handsome with chiseled cheekbones and impeccable style. Jurica always looked like he was going to a business meeting, even in his casual clothing. He was in his fifties like Lazar, but Jurica had aged well. Milos had started teaching tennis to Jurica's son, Adam, and they bonded over their shared heritage, as all Serbians seemed to do.

Milos liked to say, "We stick together, as friends, as family, as a culture."

The first time I met Jurica and his family was when he invited Milos and I to his house for dinner. His wife, Mara, was Swedish and a former model. She was also twenty years younger than her lawyer husband, as they had gotten married when she was eighteen. Mara was a natural blonde with an adorable bob haircut. She looked like one of the girls from shampoo commercials, with a little extra help. It was Beverly Hills after all—lip fillers, Botox, and injections were rampant.

She was also painfully skinny. The norm in her social circle.

It was strange because Mara and I were the same age, but she seemed older. More reserved. Jurica was loud and confident, while his wife preferred Rodeo Drive and solitude. I just chalked it up to being shy. One thing was obvious: how much she loved her children. Adam looked just like her, but tall like Jurica. He was your typical teenage boy. Acne and crude jokes. His hobbies included airsoft guns and video games.

Their daughter Emma and I were instant friends. She was only nine, but wise well beyond her years. Long, black curly hair hung down her back, a complement to her warm brown eyes. She was her father's child, only her straight, thin nose a twin to Mara's. Emma was just precious. It was odd to be having adult conversations with a tiny human, who escorted me all over their home, showing me her science kit and singing and playing songs on her miniature piano.

They lived in Beverly Hills, so their digs were excessive to say the least. A two-story modern box that Jurica had designed himself. The inside was white and metal, with large windows, and sterile. You could have eaten off their floors, they were so clean. All the furniture looked futuristic and wasn't designed for comfort.

"Do you want to see my sticker collection?" little Emma proclaimed, dragging me into her bedroom.

Her room was just as clean as the rest of the house, but with a princess vibe. Pink curtains on the windows and a frilly pink bedspread. No toys were visible; everything was put away in tubs in the closet. Speaking of her closet, the designer clothes were meticulously arranged. Many of the items with tags still intact. Ralph Lauren, Burberry, and so on. Mara had a passion for fashion and used her husband's credit cards with abandon.

"You have beautiful dresses, Emma!" I proclaimed, sitting on the floor with her while she pulled out her treasure box from under her bed.

"They're okay, I guess. Want a flower or a heart?" She held up two sticker sheets, both well-used with only a few still attached.

"Heart, please!"

Emma peeled it off and stuck it to my face, which made us both laugh.

The dynamics at our first dinner with Jurica and his family were interesting. I have always watched human interactions and body language, and I was usually pretty good at picking up on the temperature of relationships. Mara was quiet, barely picking at the food that their cook had prepared, as Jurica described the palace he was building in Montenegro. Not once did they look at each other or make any bodily contact. It was obvious that their marriage was strained.

So started my Serbian social circle.

There were weekly soccer games at their Orthodox Church. Lazar would be in attendance, as well as Jurica and his family.

Emma and I would chat away or play word game apps on my phone as we watched the boys scream and kick around the ball.

Mara, try as I might, kept her sunglasses on and her distance.

It was now December, and Milos hadn't talked to his mother, Zora, in months.

Christmas was fast approaching, my favorite holiday, and work was even busier. Usually, brands have certain budgets for advertising around that time and I was slammed. Lui had lost another ten pounds—to my delight—and was a whole new dog. Proper nutrition and exercise had turned him into a sleek thing of beauty.

Lui and I were two peas in a pod, but Milos was another story.

Our fights were becoming a weekly occurrence. My love was still under a ton of pressure, and had fallen into a pattern of ranting at me...which was unfortunate. I know you usually take things out on the ones you love, but I was growing tired of his blow-ups and apologies.

Good news, Milos had taken his third board exam and passed. The medical board lets you take the tests out of order, with step three being an in-person exam with actors pretending to be patients. By far the easiest of the three, according to Milos.

Still having to complete USMLE step one and step two, both of which were multiple choice, my foreign doctor was beyond overwhelmed. In California, you have to pass your medical board exams and be board-certified before starting a medical residency. He was behind schedule, but Doctor Lancaster had given him an extra month to finish.

We were in a delicate place. The last thing we needed was what came next.

A few days before Christmas, Milos received a call from Nikola.

It was a chilly morning, and I was in my bathrobe, scratching Lui's head as he leaned against my leg. My other free hand invariably typed at my computer. Milos was on the phone in the living room, out of sight as his voice started to rise. Of course, speaking in Serbian, so I had no clue what was being said.

He hung up, marched into my office, and started pacing.

"My mother is on a plane. Nikola said she is coming to see why I am wasting my life. This is fucking bullshit!" he yelled, running his hands through his hair in frustration. "I cannot be in a relationship and have her here. She is planning to stay as long as it takes for me to come to my senses!"

To be honest, I saw the writing on the wall. If I was in her shoes, and had a son who had run away to another country, stayed away for two years, and then decided to move there permanently because of some female, I would probably have been on a plane a whole lot sooner.

A little tidbit I have failed to mention: Milos didn't exactly leave Serbia with their blessing. He had packed a suitcase and exited in the middle of the night. Sick of their control and plans for his life, he had basically run away from home.

According to Milos, he spent his first month in the United States at a hotel room at the W in Hollywood. My playboy had come with over seven hundred thousand dollars in the bank, just to blow. In his mind, he had worked extremely hard in medical school and had earned a well-deserved vacation.

I don't think he intended to stay away for so long, but the more time he spent in America, the more he wasn't ready to give up his freedom just yet.

"She can stay with us? I have the fold-out bed in the TV room?" I offered.

My house had three bedrooms: one for sleep, one that I had converted into a closet office, and the smallest room, which contained a TV and a white sleeper sofa that Lui had semi-destroyed.

"Absolutely not. One moment." Milos dialed a number on his phone, held it to his ear, and waited.

"Jurica, hi. How are you?" he said as he exited again, a plan already forming.

It was time I met the infamous Zora.

Chapter 6

BETRAYAL

My house was clean? Check. Flowers and presents for my potential, future mother-in-law? Check. Conservative makeup and clothing that screamed, "I'm a good thing for your son!"? One sec, yup, check!

My life motto has always been, "You love me, you just don't know it yet!" For the most part, it usually works. I just keep being myself and persistently friendly until you succumb to my nerdy charm. My strategy with Zora was going to be no different. I genuinely loved her son and was sure I would grow to love her. All I needed was for her to give me a chance.

Milos had gone to pick up his giver-of-life at LAX, as she was getting in late. I had insisted that he pick her up alone, praying that the drive would give them some time to talk, and hopefully smooth things over as much as possible.

It felt like our first date, nervous anxiety overwhelming me as I waited on the couch.

I was lost in thought when my awful doorbell rang, startling me back into the moment. Milos was peeking in the window beside the front door. A smile on his face as he indicated for me to open to it, even though he had a key.

This was a good sign.

Bracing myself for the worst, I grabbed the handle and swung open the door to reveal Zora.

My eyes met hers, and I tried not to laugh.

She was tiny, only maybe five feet, and as wide as she was tall. Her hair was cropped close in a pixie cut, and dyed a bright red. I could not believe that Milos was terrified of this creature. She reminded me of Suki from *Gilmore Girls*, seemingly harmless. Not the powerhouse business woman Milos had described.

He had showed me photos of her when she was younger and had told me that she had quit smoking and was having some weight issues, but to say the least, I was shocked.

A pointy chin was nestled in a bed of fat, toad-like in its appearance. Even more painfully obvious was the large, hairy mole on the left side of her mouth. I kept staring at her as Milos happily chatted away, your typical first-time introductions and small talk.

They literally looked nothing alike, except for the nose. A stranger would never guess that they were related, let alone that Milos was her child.

Please don't think I'm shallow. I'm just describing her physically as I saw her in that moment.

But her smile was warm as I went in for a hug, and her clothes were tailored and expensive. Milos had explained that she used to be quite fluent in English from her own times spent in the States, but I would just have to speak slowly.

All three of us, and Lui, sat on the couch. She seemed to enjoy the new blanket I bought her, and the flowers. Lui was excited for a fresh body in the house, and kept pestering her, to her dismay.

"*Smrdljivi pas!*" she exclaimed as he tried to hump her leg.

Milos was no help, in stiches over his horny dog's antics.

I tried my best to tell her a little about myself. Milos kept looking at me with tenderness, winking as he held my hand. Zora's sharp brown eyes were calculating, watching how Milos and I interacted. She was pleasant, and if I had to put a read on how things were going, I think that I wasn't what she had expected.

It was getting close to midnight, and try as I might, I couldn't hide the yawns.

Taking the hint, Milos obliged.

"Come, Mama, I will take you to Jurica's."

Turns out that Zora and Jurica were already friends from before he left Belgrade, where she now resided. Milos insisted that Zora was going to stay with Jurica and his family, as they had a huge house with multiple guest rooms.

I think Milos wanted some distance from his mother as well. He had told me that I was his first real relationship, and he didn't want her interfering.

More hugs were exchanged, they left, and I prayed that things were off to a good start.

Lui agreed that it was time for bed, as his snores rumbled from the kitchen long before I had my face washed and my teeth brushed. Just as I rolled back the covers, Milos's headlights and the sound of his car parking told me I wouldn't be hitting the hay quite yet.

I sat on my bed, waiting, as my gorgeous male specimen entered. He was still smiling, his shoulders relaxed in a baggy grey hoodie.

"Do you want to know what my mother said the moment that we left?" he asked.

Do pigs like mud? Kind of a rhetorical question, but the suspense was killing me.

"Please do tell!" I cooed, sleepy but on edge.

"She said, 'I get it! You have my blessing.' She adores you."

Phew. Passed the Mom test. Hallelujah!

I looked at the freckles on his face, the dimples in his cheeks, his red full lips, and five o'clock shadow. I looked at his muscular arms and strong physique. I looked at his big blue eyes and right into his soul. I looked at the man on the inside, hardworking and complex, passionate and mysterious. I really looked at the man before me, and I fell in love all over again.

The next morning felt like a turning point in our relationship. We had been through so much already in the seven months we had been together, and with Zora's blessing, there really could be a future for us.

I fully expected a proposal at any moment.

Milos had hinted before that, when Milos decided to marry, Nikola had offered to buy the engagement ring. In the past, I had never cared about this kind of stuff. Never planned my wedding as a little girl, or pictured what kind of dress I was going to wear, or how I would style my hair.

If I wanted to irritate my parents, all I had to do was mention how "when I find 'the one' I am going to Vegas and eloping." I just didn't understand the whole wedding part. If you found someone that you loved and wanted to be with, why wait, and why spend a small fortune to get the ball rolling?

Back to rings. I didn't care what size, style, or kind of engagement ring, I just wanted it to be official. I was his, he was mine, and if he wanted to get me a ring from a quarter machine, I would have worn it with pride.

Christmas for me always meant thoughtful presents. Crazy as this might sound, Milos wanted a gun. He was in the army in Serbia for a year, so I wasn't concerned with him knowing how to properly handle a weapon. My house in Highland Park wasn't exactly in the best neighborhood. An actual, real live drug dealer lived a few doors down, so I didn't think it would hurt.

Milos did some research, found a Colt handgun that he wanted in a gun shop in Glendale, and I went with him to check it out. We came, we saw, we bought a gun, we paid a deposit, Milos had to fill out the necessary paperwork, and then we had to wait for him to pick it up.

The timing was kind of perfect, because my mom was coming into town for Christmas as well! She had already met Milos twice before, and heartily approved our pairing. I felt so lucky, him liking my mom and I liking his. We could finally have peace and build on our relationship from a place of support.

But I was scrambling, trying to find something for Zora for the occasion. I hadn't expected to have to get a gift for her as well.

My mother, Barbara, has endless energy, so she accompanied me to the mall on the morning of Christmas Eve.

"What do you want to get her?" Mom asked, walking arm in arm with me at the Americana mall in Glendale. It was just the two of us, as Milos was giving us a chance to catch up, and time for him to find Zora a gift as well.

Unlike Milos and Zora, I was my mother's clone. Only a few inches taller, and my hair blown straight. Hers was a beautiful mess of curls, grey hairs blending with dark. My mom was, and is, classic elegance.

"Ugh, I have no clue. What do you buy someone who owns part of an island?"

As I had mentioned before, Milos's mother had gifted her son with property in Montenegro, right on the ocean. That multi-million dollar project was only a smidgen of his inheritance, a tiny speck of Zora's vast fortune.

"Well, what does she like?" she said, trying to help me with this particular puzzle.

"Me, hopefully."

We both laughed. I inherited my sense of humor from her.

I settled on snatching up a coin pouch that matched the purse I saw Zora wearing a few nights prior. It cost a small fortune, as the bag was Gucci, but I love giving gifts and watching the reactions, especially when the present is well thought-out.

It was the kind of gift that said, "I am observant and I care."

Plus, if she was going to be my second mom, might as well treat her as I did my own.

I was right—my present was a hit. We were at Jurica's house that evening, planning to introduce Barbara and Zora to each other and celebrate our first Christmas together. Their cook had gone all out: turkey and various holiday dishes littered the table. To my feigned annoyance, I was no longer Emma's favorite.

She told my mother, in detail, about her boyfriend at school. Grabbing her cellphone, she recited their text message conversations, going so far as to hunt down her school yearbook and point out every page that he was on.

My childhood boyfriend was *Home Improvement* star Jonathan Taylor Thomas, and only in my mind. Emma had mad game.

After dinner, we exchanged presents. Serbian Orthodox Christmas is on January 7, so Jurica and his family had no preference if we opened our packages on Christmas Eve or Christmas Day. My family has always opted for Christmas Eve, so that was that.

Zora, with tears in her eyes, held up the small piece of leather I had painstakingly purchased. Wrapping paper and various items cluttered the normally sterile dining room. Many opened gifts lay on the table between us, dangerously close to the remaining food items.

"Brittani, many thanks, very nice," she said, struggling to communicate her unexpected joy. She kissed my cheeks, then she hugged my mom as well before returning to the other side of the table and the seat next to her son.

My gift from Milos was equally thoughtful. He had custom ordered a black messenger bag from a designer in Portland, Oregon. I already had one of her purses, and I was always going on about how I wanted to add to my budding collection.

No need to give you a list of all the items given or received that night, but you get the idea.

Jurica was his normal, boisterous self. Mara, her normal, gorgeous, mute, and slightly plastic-looking self.

Try as I might, I couldn't take my eyes off of Milos. He had on a white button-down shirt and grey dress pants, paired with a black belt and dress shoes. Jurica was telling some funny story about Lazar, how he had taken his former father-in-law to Mexico for his bachelor party and then lost him, only to find him the next day at a hotel with three hookers and a donkey.

Not the most appropriate story for the occasion, but how he was rehashing it had us all in stiches.

Milos rubbed the stubble on his strong jaw, enthralled by Jurica's rendition. I think he was drawn to Jurica because he was old enough to be his dad. I had never heard him say it out loud, but I could see that he longed for some form of a fatherly role model.

After dinner, we all moved to the sterile living room. The house was devoid of decorations, except for a giant Christmas tree with lights shoved in one corner. Not a single ornament dangling from its branches. It should have softened the room, but it was just as bare and severe as the rest of the dwelling.

If you had been a stranger looking at the group of us, trying to sit on the couches, the only word to use is comical. There was a lot of fidgeting, and shifting, but it didn't stunt the conversation.

It was Milos's turn to tell a funny story. A few days earlier, he had been walking Lui by our house and one of my neighbors had stopped him. She proceeded to give him a lecture about how he should neuter his dog, if he was a responsible pet owner.

"Oh no, that is a tumor. Poor thing, he doesn't have very long left to live. I have just been cuddling and holding him a lot," Milos had said.

Her angry features turned to horror, broken up about Lui and his balls.

"I am...so sorry, poor thing!" she stuttered, not knowing how to recover from her blunder.

We erupted into laughter, and Jurica wiped away tears as he threw his arm around his somber wife. Mara and Emma were the only ones not doubled over. Mara lacked a sense of humor, and Emma didn't quite grasp the joke.

Trying to avoid another late night, it was sadly time for us to say our goodbyes.

My handsome foreigner walked my mom and me to my car. He was going to stay the night at Jurica's and spend Christmas morning with Zora, Jurica, and his family.

Right on cue, my very observant mother gave Milos a hug and made herself scarce, disappearing into the front passenger side of my Mini Cooper, pretending to be engrossed in her text messages.

"I love you, Brittani," Milos said, hugging me tight as he whispered in my ear.

"I love you, Milos."

What I hate about life is that, the moment I seem to get to a point where I am truly happy, invariably something happens to take away my thunder.

Something painful, like my father's passing. Something that can shake me to my very core.

A few days later, my mother returned home to Sedona, Arizona. She was only able to make short trips, since her horses and gardens kept her on a tight leash. I was sad to see her go, and I had enjoyed watching her and Zora bond.

Still on a high from Christmas, New Year's Eve was just as magical. Spending it yet again at Jurica's, this time with an onslaught of additional bodies, mostly Serbian and from their church soccer league, with everyone's plus-ones.

I was happy, I was in love, and I was ready to talk about how happy and in love I was with anyone that would listen. Starting with Snapchat.

"Take a photo with me!" I was sitting on Milos's lap, yet again on Mara's white leather couch. Voices resonated, louder than they should have from the copious amounts of liquor and general jubilation that surrounded ringing in the New Year.

I was the only sober one there; Milos was buzzed, but still fairly lucid.

"What kind of photo?" he said, biting my ear.

"Stop, hold still, and smile!"

Wrapping his arms around me, I snapped a quick picture. Added some sort of generic caption like "Happy 2016!" and sent it to "my story." Now, a portion of my internet audience that followed me on that particular app would know something was up.

January 2, 2016

I wasn't done sharing yet. I filmed and uploaded a YouTube video, wanting to spill the beans and be able to be honest about how I was feeling. Talking about personal struggles and dealing with life setbacks. The grand finale was my big reveal. I, Brittani Louise Taylor, was in a relationship, and Lui wasn't really my dog, he was Milos's.

It felt like a huge weight off my chest! I no longer had to take photos alone and pretend like he didn't exist in my work life. Wanting to make sure I had my partner's approval in outing us, I had Milos watch the video before uploading. He gave me the green light, so I took the plunge.

We were in this together.

I remember hanging out that afternoon. It was a Saturday, and the both of us lounged in my back bedroom. Milos was in between his tennis lessons and had a few hours to kill. I was working on a script for filming that evening. It involved The Magic Castle in Hollywood, a magician, and a shout-out promoting a new television show.

Oddly typical for me.

I had also booked a job hosting for a well-known car brand at the Detroit Auto Show, and I had a flight early the next morning.

So basically, I was going to film, edit like a banshee, turn in the video for approval minus effects, and sleep on the plane.

Milos's phone started to ring. Upon seeing the caller's identity on his screen, he jumped up and left the room to answer.

Minutes passed. Expecting to hear him speaking Serbian, or Russian, I instead heard English.

"Calm down, you don't want to do this," he said, an edge to his tone. A few more moments went by. "Fine."

He must have hung up, but he didn't return to the room right away. I watched him walk into the kitchen, stop, turn the other direction and take a few steps, stopping again. Even from my spot on the couch, I could plainly see that he was visibly shaking.

"What is going on?" I said, immediately closing my laptop.

He walked into the back bedroom and right in front of me. Stopped. All color drained from his face. Took a few steps to leave, stopped.

Now I was really worried.

"I need to tell you something." Milos rubbed the stubble on his chin, frustrated.

"Fine, tell me. What is going on?"

My instincts told me not to approach him. Let him open up on his own, at his own pace.

"When I met you, I wanted to stay. I had to stay."

We had been over this before, none of it was new news.

"What you didn't know is that I did something, so I could stay, so I could be with you!"

Let me guess, you got married? I didn't voice that out loud, but I think I knew where this was headed.

"You know Oksana, right? My Russian friend?"

He had mentioned her before. Milos was friends with her son, Paul, and he knew both of them through Nikola. Oksana was an old client of Nikola's furniture business when she was still living in Russia.

"You know how she is married, right? In Russia? Well she did me a favor. I gave her my last one hundred and seventy thousand dollars for her to marry me here, so I could get a green card."

I hate it when I am right.

Ouch. But I was silent. Trying to wrap my mind around what he had just revealed.

"I met you, I had to stay! My student visa was expiring, I was going back to Serbia. But, I loved you. You told me you had just gotten out of a relationship with someone who was paid to marry a girl for her green card. I didn't want you to hate me, because I did the same, except I was the one paying."

It was kind of romantic, in a seriously messed up way. He had met me, fallen in love, given every last penny to get a piece of plastic that said he could stay, so he could keep pursuing me.

"So, I have been dating a married man?" I asked, my face strained into a smile, still in shock.

"There is more, Brittani," Milos said, starting to pace again.

The next part needs a little back story.

I have mentioned Jurica and Lazar already, but they also had an infamous friend named Vladimir. According to Milos, Vlad had worked in the treasury for the Serbian government, but had stolen millions of dollars and escaped to the US. Anyone could google about Vlad and see about his pending trial, and the attempts to extradite him back.

Milos, Jurica, Lazar, and Vlad would frequent an expensive steak house in Hollywood once a week, for male bonding and full bellies. Vlad would often text or call Milos for medical advice, the paranoia that went along with his situation making him physically ill. At this point, Milos had even roped in Doctor Lancaster to help him find another doctor to write Vlad a medical letter, stating that he was "in a car accident" and "due to his injuries, was unable to fly."

Money was exchanged for that letter. Illegal? Yes.

Why illegal? Because he wasn't actually injured at all—there was no car accident. He just needed a valid reason why he couldn't travel by plane to his trial. The plan being that the medical letter would buy Vlad more time.

The sooner Milos passed his board exams, and started his residency, the better. I didn't approve of his friends and some of the choices he was making because of their influence, but I didn't feel like it was my place to tell him who he could and couldn't spend time with.

"You know how Vlad and Lazar love women. Remember when I asked you to meet me in Marina Del Rey for drinks? Before our first date?" Milos asked.

I nodded my head in acknowledgement, on the edge of my seat as to what could possibly be worse than him already being hitched.

"That night, Lazar and I met a few call girls at the bar. Lazar introduced them to Vlad, and they would sometimes join us for dinner. One of the girls, Bunny, is obsessed with me. She has been trying for months to get my attention, I keep telling her I have a girlfriend. Fucking Lazar was drunk and told Bunny about my illegal marriage, and now she is trying to blackmail me for money."

"Was that her on the phone?" I asked.

His turn to nod. The fear from moments before, turning to bitterness.

"I was going to tell you. Oksana and I have already filed for divorce, right after I got my green card. Bunny said she is going to contact you, but don't talk to her. Don't respond. I need to call Nikola."

With that, he exited the room again.

I felt like I was in some Lifetime Movie. This was not only really happening, but it was literally insane.

What did I do? Picked up my laptop, continued to work. Waited.

I had no clue what to do in that moment, what to think. I was just stunned.

Milos came back in, fresh off a phone call with Nikola.

"He is going to take care of it," Milos stated, dead serious.

"How can Nikola take care of this? He is in Serbia."

"He has his connections."

"Milos, he deals in chairs and light fixtures. What could he possibly do?"

Pacing again, great, more to be revealed.

"Nikola deals in furniture, yes, but he does more. He is high up in the Serbian mafia."

What. The. Hell.

My brain was totally and completely overloaded. Married, blackmail, and now mafia? I wanted to run out my front door and keep running. I did not sign up for this. My face must have spoken volumes, because Milos was instantly beside me.

"Brittani, Brittani, listen to me." Milos took my laptop off my lap and set it on the table. Sitting down next to me, he grabbed my hands, pleading.

"I am no longer involved, I am here, I am with you. I just want to do my medicine."

My brain started to work again, words were forming, so many questions that needed to be answered. "What do you mean, he will take care of it? You aren't going to kill her, are you?"

"No, no, we don't kill women. Even if she is a greedy slut, he will just send a few people to talk to her."

Again, more questions. "What do you mean, 'talk to her,' exactly?"

"Just make her understand that there will be consequences if she doesn't stop."

Dark, brooding. This new side of Milos scared me. I knew he had a past, but this was just too much.

The alarm on my phone went off, startling me further. Whether I liked it or not, I had to get ready and head to my shoot. Contracts were signed, there was a deadline, and I had to deliver.

I honestly don't remember what Milos said to me as he helped me carry my clothes to the car and kissed me, reassuring me that everything was going to be fine.

The rest of the evening was a daze. Foggy, on autopilot, I smiled and worked. Pretending that everything was great as the cameras rolled. Before I knew it, we were done. Not wanting any more trauma, I had turned my phone off for the duration of that evening.

Back in my car, I was brave enough to switch it back on. It powered up and I was met with a flood of texts from Milos checking on my well-being, emails with my itinerary for Detroit, updated hosting scripts, and two emails from Bunny.

I stopped breathing. The title of Bunny's first email was "He's Lying...."

My heart pounded. How did she find my email address? I mean, it was on my social media for business purposes. That must be it.

I am going to paraphrase the main email, because it was long, but it basically said the following:

"He's lying. He told me that you were just some girl who took care of his dog, and would never let me meet you, which I thought was odd. He would only call me from the car, and we would go on dates with Lazar, Vlad, and Jurica. I have more proof if you need it."

Attached were forty-plus screenshots. Text messages that were supposedly between them, photos of Milos, photos of Lui. Tinder messages. I wanted to vomit.

As I read and re-read her emails, I started sobbing.

My chest was heaving. I could barely talk as I dialed my mom and explained everything to her—Milos's revelations, Bunny, Nikola. The first thing she said was, "I am going to get in the car and start driving."

It is roughly eight hours from Sedona to LA, and I had no choice but to go to Detroit the following day.

"Mom, I have to finish editing and catch a plane tomorrow."

"Honey, I know. But what can I do? I talked to Milos earlier, I believe him. He is really, really upset. Have you tried to call him?"

My brain was so emotionally overloaded that I wasn't thinking straight. Milos. He was probably desperate and might do something rash. I should try to contact him.

"I am going to call you back, I love you."

"Please, let me know how I can help. Love you more!" she hung up, as I dialed the accused.

It took three tries before he answered. His voice made it clear he had been crying as well.

"Hello, Brittani."

"Milos, where are you?" I demanded. The fact that I was unreachable for five hours while on set might have sent him into a tailspin.

"You have to believe me. I am going to kill myself if you don't believe me. Brittani, I didn't do this. You have to believe me!"

He kept repeating himself, the very definition of despair.

"Where are you? Milos, are you at home?"

He hung up.

I should have gotten a speeding ticket as I raced back, recklessly pushing traffic laws. Pulling up to my house, Milos's car wasn't there.

Panic set in.

Turning around, I headed back down my street when I spotted his brown BMW stopped on the left side of the road. Hitting my brakes, I parked across from it and rushed out. Running to his car door, his head was on the wheel.

Fearing the worst, I knocked on the window.

He looked up at me, disoriented, his eyes puffy from crying. Thank God, he was okay.

"Open the door," I said through the glass.

He obliged, lethargic from total devastation.

I held his hand and attempted to soothingly rub his shoulders. Trying to calm him down.

"Come home," I said.

He collected himself and followed me back, Jurica's sleek Mercedes pulled up out front. Milos must have called him. He also rushed out, relieved as well at seeing that Milos was okay.

Now that was a good friend. Jurica was in the middle of a huge court battle with a celebrity that was caught shoplifting, it was all over the news. Still, he had dropped everything to come help a friend in need.

We all gathered in my kitchen, since none of us felt like sitting. Milos and I were silent, Jurica and him on one side of the center island, and I on the other.

Never had I felt more alone than I did in that moment.

"Brittani, she is a hooker. But you have every right to dump Milos. He was stupid for hanging out with us, he knew what she was after. You should dump him!" said Jurica, world's worst giver of advice.

But he was trying!

"Thank you for coming," I said, "but what I think I need to do now is talk to Milos, alone."

Jurica shifted from one foot to another, ready to leave, but also worried and wanting to stay and help.

"He loves you, Brittani."

"I know, thank you again."

We walked him to the door. Jurica gave me an awkward hug and clapped Milos on the back.

"If you need anything, you call me!" he said to Milos, making it clear that he meant it.

After he left, what do I do? Headed to the office and hooked up my hard drives, wanting to edit and focus on anything else but what had just transpired.

Milos needed me, but I needed to sit down.

He followed me from room to room, like his puppy. Milos crumpled to the floor in my office-closet and started crying again, as Lui tried to give him a tongue bath. Lui hated licking, he thought humans tasted terrible, but he was trying to do something to comfort his owner.

My tears had dried up. I could have cried all night, but again, I had a deadline to meet and Milos was going to have to talk to me while I worked.

And he did talk, for hours, my mother calling or texting and checking on us as well, worried sick.

Here is what Milos had surmised.

"The photos in the texts, that Bunny used, I sent those to Lazar. Bunny and him have been sleeping together for a while, she could have easily gotten them off his phone. And look, look at the photos of us all together, I am so uncomfortable. See? She is all over me! She has been planning this," Milos said.

I was listening, but also sifting through footage from the shoot earlier, wanting to crawl into a hole and self-destruct.

"She used an app, see the conversations? I don't even talk like this. 'Baby'? I don't call anyone 'baby'! She is so crazy! I wouldn't date that hobbit!"

He grabbed his laptop and proceeded to pull up multiple sites and show me how you can generate text message conversations that look real.

"This is how she did it! Brittani, you have to believe me! I gave up everything to be with you!"

His voice broke.

I couldn't handle anymore crying, I knew he was right, but I couldn't help feeling like I was cheated on. I felt like I had been betrayed.

Someone was intentionally trying to hurt me. To hurt us.

Someone was intentionally trying to hurt my relationship.

How could anyone be so evil?

Chapter 7

BUN IN THE OVEN

I was a glutton for punishment. Sitting on the plane on my flight to Detroit, I had purchased the wi-fi just so I could keep reading Bunny's emails over and over. My eyes were strained from the computer screen. Barely blinking, I wanted to pick out all the discrepancies, I wanted to see the story she crafted in her head. Maybe if I looked at them long enough, it would dull the annoying pain that kept washing over me in waves.

Again, I felt like I had been cheated on. When I hadn't. Ugh.

This woman was obviously insane. She had created a fake relationship. She had decided that she wanted Milos. She was just another Beverly Hills husband hunter trying to get hitched and rich.

When he rejected her, she decided that she was going to make him pay.

It was almost good that I had three days to clear my head. My hosting job was extremely demanding: not only did I have to memorize six very wordy scripts, but my co-host and I had to interact with a giant computer screen while delivering our lines. Each night, back at the hotel, was the only real time I had to think.

When I was alone, that was the worst part. Sure, I talked to Milos on the phone. He surmised that Lazar was also in on Bunny's scheme and he was furious. Milos believed that Lazar knew about his inheritance, and that Lazar and Bunny were more than likely planning to split whatever hush cash they hoped to gain.

I knew he was sketchy.

And mafia? Really? According to Milos, when he said he had "left the family business," he wasn't kidding.

"I never killed anyone, beat a few people up, sure. Some owed Nikola money or were trying to step in on his territory. Never drugs, some smuggling, some money laundering," he had told me.

"And Zora? Is she involved too?"

Milos sighed, but answered my question. "Love, my whole family is part of it. That is how we survived, after the war. You don't understand how things were. We had no choice."

Milos was so casual as he delved into his past. The cat really was out of the bag.

If I had known about Milos's family when I first met him, I would have run for the hills. The problem now was that I was in too deep. He had my heart. Milos said he was a product of circumstance. He didn't choose to be born into his family any more than I chose to have webbed feet.

Kidding. About my feet.

My grandfather always said you have to play the card that you are dealt.

Their plethora of legal and illegal operations had made Zora, Nikola, and all of the Mihajlovics extremely wealthy. That kind of money bought friends in high places, all over the world. Moral of the story, stay on their good side. It was obviously lucrative, as it had financed Milos's medical school, fancy cars, and lavish vacations. But it was blood money and Milos had gotten out.

Is the arms dealer as guilty as the hand that pulls the trigger? Absolutely.

But Milos had chosen a fresh start, long before he and I had connected. That was admirable.

Was marrying Oksana stupid? Yes. But at that moment, it was the least of my worries.

"Brittani, I tried to make Milos tell you. We have argued much. He loves you, I know my son. That girl, he didn't do this," Zora stated, taking the phone from Milos.

She was still staying at Jurica's home. Milos was there as well, camped out with Lui in their guest house and studying for his board exams. He didn't want to be alone, and Jurica had offered.

I thanked Zora for her support, then she put Milos back on. "Jurica, is he mafia as well?"

I had to ask.

"Most of my friends are. That is why they know me, and my family. Zora and Nikola are very well respected in Serbia."

Things were starting to make more sense. At the Orthodox church we frequented, the property was surrounded by a massive iron gate, security cameras, and two armed guards. Seemed like overkill or paranoia. I mean, they were just playing soccer...right?

Are you freaking out? Because I sure was.

It came down to this. There were two choices. One, break up with him and try to find someone with normal issues, like not being happy in their career or having back hair. Or two, stay with him, accept that his family was dangerous but steer clear of anything illegal, and carve out our own path together.

I picked option number two.

He was my person. Girls always like bad boys, right? Or former bad boys.

Heading back to Los Angeles from Detroit, I was determined. This hussy wasn't going to win, she wasn't going to ruin anything. Milos was mine and I was his, period.

A few days after I returned, Milos and I were lying in bed after a morning romp. We were both being clingy, not wanting to let the other out of our sight.

"You are basically already my wife," he said.

I laughed, because it was true. "Oh yeah, how so?"

"We are pretty much married, we just need to actually get married. One lifetime with you isn't enough."

Not the proposal that I had expected, but romantic. Even if the moment was bittersweet.

"Sure, let's do it."

Milos laughed, rolling me to my back with his muscular arms and kissing me.

"I didn't want to pick out a ring, because I wanted you to come with me. Nikola already said he will pay for it."

With that, we were engaged. Kind of.

I should have been blissfully happy. The man of my dreams wanted to be stuck with me for eternity. But it didn't help that I found Bunny's Instagram. She had tagged me in two photos of her and Milos. The same photos she had already emailed to me and then decided to post on her social media. Aggravating.

Another blow: Milos had to turn down the medical residency at FHH. They had given him until the end of January to complete step one and step two. He tried his best to study, when he wasn't teaching tennis, but there just weren't enough hours in the day.

If all that we had been going through wasn't overwhelming enough, there was even more drama at Jurica's home.

Part of Milos's time issue was also Mara. Jurica had left for Europe for a month, supposedly for business and to supervise construction on their house in Spain. Mara stayed home, with their two kids and Zora.

What Jurica had failed to disclose was that Mara was an alcoholic.

Practically every night, Mara would get piss drunk and fall down. Zora would then try to haul her into bed and then hunt down her stashes while her children screamed and cried. Emma and Adam caught the worst of it.

Now, when Milos wasn't teaching tennis, he was at Jurica's house trying to wrangle Mara. It was such a mess.

Whatever free time I had was spent distracting Emma, or playing video games with Adam, as their mother sank lower and lower into a cycle of substance abuse.

Her downward spiral was not unwarranted. There was definitely a reason why Mara was imploding. She poured her heart out to Zora night after night. About how Jurica had been cheating on her most of their marriage. His infidelity and indifference had made her turn to self-medicating and self-loathing. He was her entire world. She wanted her husband, but he didn't want her.

I felt for Mara, and I was furious with Jurica for burying his head in the sand. Milos was loyal to his friends, even if their actions were despicable.

It was now early February 2016. A very tired Milos and I decided to hit up a flea market in Pasadena, taking a much-needed moment of respite. Nestled in the thick of various tents, each boasting their wares, we decided to divide and conquer. Milos browsed the old records while I hunted for a new nightstand to go next to my bed.

No luck. But it was a beautiful day, and I was enjoying the outdoor air beneath my sun hat. Milos was in a foul mood, disgruntled with life in general.

"All I need is two months. Two months of uninterrupted studying to pass my boards," he said.

"Why don't you just do it? Stop teaching tennis, buckle down?"

He laughed bitterly.

"Yes, and how am I going to pay my bills? Make car payments? Lui's food? All I want to do is medicine, heal. The universe is punishing me."

"What if I helped you out? For two months? I will pick up all the bills. You, just study."

I could tell he was resistant to the idea, a gentleman who wanted to pay his own way, but I was persistent.

"Think about if the situation was reversed and I needed financial help? Would you make the same offer?"

"Brittani, if I had money, you wouldn't be paying for a thing."

"Exactly, so why don't you let me help you, and when you pass your boards and get your surgery residency, you're my sugar daddy!"

It took a few hours of persistence, but he finally gave in.

My hosting job with a major car manufacturer continued into March. This time, for two weeks in New York at the International Auto Show. I was not only excited for the opportunity, but the income. Being the sole bread winner was getting to be expensive.

Jurica finally returned from his European escapades, and stuck Mara into rehab. Zora, no longer concerned about her son and exhausted from babysitting Mara, caught the first plane she could back to Belgrade.

Finally, Milos and I were alone and back on track, but all of the strain had taken a toll.

I felt like I loved him, but I didn't know if I was in love. Not anymore. It wasn't fair—our relationship had had to endure more than most people go through in a lifetime and then some.

It was a relief to be in New York, alone.

My hotel was in Manhattan, and I loved walking to the Javits Center and back each day, choosing to avoid public transportation. I loved the high rises, potholes, taxis, and general chaos that makes up a largely populated city. Most of my other co-workers were counting down the days, sick of being locked up in a convention center hour after hour.

If anything, I was dreading my trip ending. I didn't want to go back to my life, because I was sick of my life.

I didn't miss Milos. I loved our time apart.

I equated our relationship with stress.

That was when I realized what I needed to do. When I got back to LA, we needed to take a break. I needed room to breathe, to digest, to really figure out if he was my soulmate or just someone to lust after.

That was the worst part about love, discovering that what you had had was no more. One too many fights, or crossed wires, and feelings had disappeared. Now that I had made a decision, the emotional stress was also causing me physical stress. I was having a hard time eating, suffering from indigestion and acne. I was a wreck.

My period was also five days late, which never happens.

Before I knew it, I was back in LA, back in my home with Lui and Milos.

Knowing what I needed to do wasn't making things any easier, especially when Milos was trying so hard to hang on. Even the thought of hurting him stopped my tongue. The more I put it off, the more wound up I became. It didn't help that my lady parts were still not cooperating.

Wait. Could I be pregnant? No.

Pregnancy test? Couldn't hurt.

Did I order a pack of twenty-five test strips from Amazon? Yup.

Did I pee on five before believing the results? Oh yeah.

No sooner was the tiny strip in my urine before it indicated a positive.

I was pregnant.

Well, shit.

Talk about, by far, the biggest shock of my life. I used to always joke that I was going to freeze my eggs, and right before they were going to expire, *maybe* think about having children. Kids are amazing, I love kids, I just didn't know if I wanted kids of my very own.

I'm observant. I had seen my friends' lives change with offspring; I knew what a huge commitment being a parent was. I was terrified.

Why, universe? Why now? Especially when I was ready to walk away.

There was so much that I wanted to do, that I wanted to accomplish before taking this kind of step. In my mind, if I ever did have a child, I would be married, financially stable, and hecka old.

On the couch in the back bedroom where most of our drama seemed to occur, I told Milos the news. He sat, bewildered. Silent for no fewer than five minutes. I also sat, hysterical.

This was his fault.

Before you're like, *girl please*, let me explain.

Milos was a doctor. Right when we first started sleeping together, I asked him about pregnancy prevention. I kept asking, on a regular basis, if we should be using protection. Or if I should be on birth control. It kept feeling wrong, and being the type A personality that I am, I just couldn't let it go.

His answer was always the same. "As long as I pull out, there is no need. From a medical standpoint, it is hard enough for two healthy partners that are actually trying to have a child. We are safe."

Wrong. So, so wrong.

"This is a good thing," he finally proclaimed, coming to his own conclusion.

Tears freely fell down my cheeks as I made him leave so I could call my mom and tell her the unhappy news.

She knew that I wanted to wait until marriage, and I hadn't before disclosed to her that Milos and I had been "getting it on." My mom and I are close, but I never, ever wanted to be having a discussion about my sex life.

"Children are miracles, you will see," my mom told me. "Your son or daughter is going to be the best thing that ever happened to you guys! And I promise, I will help you raise this blessing. I am not disappointed in you! Maybe a little surprised, but this is a good thing!"

Both Milos and my mom thought this was good, so why didn't I feel the same?

I cried for three days straight. Pushing Milos away, wanting to be alone. Pregnancy hormones more than likely had something to do with my mood as well.

I felt trapped. This baby wasn't on my terms. Heck, we hadn't even been trying.

Now for a revelation that I am ashamed of.

I actually thought about not keeping the baby. Went so far as to make an appointment to end my pregnancy.

I could have lied and said that I wanted my bundle of joy from the beginning, but that just wasn't the case. I didn't see the thing growing inside of me as a person, only as an invasion. An end to my life as I knew it and tying me to Milos forever.

When it came time for my appointment, though, I just couldn't go through with it.

Like it or not, I needed to face the consequences of my stupidity.

Nineteen days into my pregnancy, I started throwing up. Lui? I couldn't be near him without vomiting. He suddenly smelled like rotten cheese to me. Milos? He had to stop wearing any kind of deodorant or aftershave, use my unscented lotion, and run an extension cord out the kitchen window so he could make coffee outside.

Never have I been so sick.

Things got a little better when I was prescribed a medication for my nausea. It was either that or be hospitalized. The drug was a class A drug, meaning no possible side effects. The stuff worked, making me queasy, but I could keep food down. One of the side effects was drowsiness. By the third pill, I could hardly keep my eyes open, so my bedtime was now 7:00 p.m.

YouTube went by the wayside.

I was so ashamed. All I wanted to do was hide, so that is what I did.

Milos left me alone in my misery. He was there if I needed him, but I pushed him away at every possible moment that I could.

During the first trimester, I had the biggest pity party on the planet. Queasy and depressed, taking prenatal vitamins and eating the proper amount of protein to keep the thing growing inside of me healthy, but that was it.

The bills started to pile up, as Milos still hadn't finished his boards.

I wanted him gone.

One morning, only a week or so away from being four months pregnant, I decided again that I was going to leave him. Marching straight into the kitchen, but not breathing because of Lui's stench, I grabbed a few extra-large trash bags and started packing up all his belongings.

Hearing me up and about, Milos came to investigate. He was wearing a white t-shirt and boxer shorts, and his head was now shaved, which made him look more severe. He must have just woken up, but I wouldn't have known as we were sleeping in separate rooms.

"What are you doing?" he asked as he marched up to me, going to grab for the trash bag.

"I am done! I am done supporting you, paying for everything! You said two months! You promised me, Milos! What has it been now? Five? Six? I want you to get out!"

Not even waiting for a response, I headed into the back bedroom where some of his books were stored.

He was getting heated. Milos heated is not a pretty sight.

"Stop this. Stop it right now." He went to grab for the trash bag and succeeded. One look at the expression on his face, and I booked it to the bathroom. I tried to close the door, but he pried it open before I even had a chance.

A wave of nausea came over me, but adrenaline had kicked in. Whatever it took, I wanted to get away from him. Milos went to grab for me, a snarl marring his normally beautiful mouth.

I started throwing anything I could reach. Shampoo bottle, soap, hair spray. It worked—he cowered as I darted past him, trying first to evade him in my office, when I remembered my cell phone was in the main bedroom. My only thought was, call the police, call 911.

Just as I was about to dial, Milos came up behind me, wrenching the phone out of my hand.

Pain erupted, but I had to get away. All I needed to do was get to my front door, and someone would hear me. Now I was running, screaming as if my life depended on it.

My neighbors that faced my living room windows were absent. The owner's wife had three small children who frequented their front yard. I hoped beyond hope that they would be playing outside, but their lawn was empty.

I didn't make it to the door before Milos had his arms around me. Overwhelming me with his strength.

"Help me! Help me! Help me!" I wailed.

My voice was raw, the sheer strain overwhelming my vocal cords. Two feet. All I had needed to make it was two feet and I would have been outside.

I kicked, I struggled, and finally I got my arm up and pushed his head away. Milos let out a howl.

"My eye! My eye! You hurt my eye!"

He bent over, one hand covering his right eye. His face, scrunched up in excruciating pain. My hand was throbbing, especially at my wrist where he had twisted it...but what had I just done?

I cautiously approached, instantly fearful that I had physically hurt him.

"Can I take a look at it?"

He grabbed his keys and wallet. "I have to go to the hospital, I can't see! I can't see! I am blind," he said.

Suddenly, I needed to sit down. Listless, on the cold wood floor, I just kept staring at my fireplace. Lui approached, whining, his clipped tail tucked between his legs.

Milos left in a flurry. Talk about conflicting emotions. He had just hurt me, but I had hurt him as well while trying to get away. I was scared, but also felt guilty. Angry, but worried.

Thankfully, the doctors thought his cornea was just bruised. His friend, Doctor Bernard, got him in with an optometrist friend, and she sent him home with an eye patch and drops.

My poor mom. After I explained what happened, she took five minutes to pack and drove straight to us, getting in at 2:00 a.m. Milos was like a son to her, and she was disappointed with me as well.

"You can't let things escalate like this. Both of you have to promise me, never, ever again. If you feel your tempers rising, just walk away. Cool off, and then calmly discuss. Whether you like it or not, you are both going to be parents. You need to grow up and fix your problems," she told us.

She was right.

Chapter 8

MOVING ON

Commence operation fresh start. Thankfully, my second trimester was more forgiving than my first. I was even able to cut back on my medication, some days not needing it at all. I still didn't look pregnant, fitting into most of my jeans even though I preferred loose dresses. Hello Spandex.

I, Brittani Taylor, was making an effort. No laying low and avoiding reality. Milos was kinder, as well. He stopped yelling and raising his voice or picking fights. Both of us were feeling guilty, and both of us were taking the necessary steps to try and repair whatever our relationship had become.

From the bad came good. Milos was almost ready to take USMLE Step One, his testing appointment scheduled for the end of June. Thankfully, his studying was lighter. Limited to online practice exams with endless potential questions.

When Milos and I had been dating for a few months, he mentioned how Nikola was trying to get some of their money out of an investment fund in Russia that had been sanctioned.

It was earning 400 percent interest, but he was unable to withdraw a penny.

He did not mention exactly how much was in the fund. Milos's share alone was well over ten billion.

Unfathomable.

Overjoyed, Milos showed me all the paperwork. Emails between Nikola and their personal banker, Sven. Sven had found another banker, Arthur, who used to work for British government. Arthur could get the money out with a 30 percent fee versus the 95 percent commission they had expected.

Nikola was making weekly trips to Switzerland to discuss the transfer of cash, as it was going to take multiple banks to be able to handle that kind of exchange. All of it made me wary. Money is great, it does relieve financial strain, but it also tends to change people.

They were estimating two months for the first payment to arrive, as it had to be done in installments. Milos's initial share was well over a hundred million.

Barely able to contain his enthusiasm, he insisted we go ring shopping. Looking at the traditional stores, nothing was really my taste. You may find it creepy, but I wanted an antique setting. Yes, my future hubby was about to be extremely loaded, but I didn't want a typical huge rock weighing down my hand.

The fun part of jewelry shopping in LA is the diamond district in Downtown. Similar to the diamond district in New York, but on a smaller scale. Even better, there were a few boutique stores that specialized in vintage finds. My nail lady had gotten her sparkler at a place called Classic Stone and gave me the push I needed to check it out.

It was now June, and Milos and I were browsing case after case of various styles and settings. Classic Stone had them organized by price range, and I was looking at engagement rings between five and ten thousand dollars. A few were promising. Simple, some filigree and modest, but high-quality diamonds.

Of course, Milos didn't like any of them.

"What about that one?" he said, pointing to the biggest and most expensive diamond in the far case.

An adorable, bubbly blonde in her early twenties hopped to his request. Melissa was nerdy hot, with her cat-eyed glasses and long straight hair. Motioning to an older gentleman behind the desk, she called in the owner of the store for backup. They must have had a company policy on the more valuable pieces to have at least two people supervising. Plus, the elderly gentlemen could haggle on the price and close the deal, as he had the final say.

Milos grabbed my hand and pulled me over, insisting that I try it on.

Of course, he was right. It was absolutely stunning. A 3.25 carat asscher with a vintage platinum mounting from the 1920s. Asschers were rare in that era, and it was a VVS2, making it much more valuable. Not a diamond expert, but all of that mumbo jumbo meant it was a stunner.

Only seventy-two thousand dollars? A steal! I mean, that is a down payment on a house. Or the price of a whole house, depending on what area on the planet that you live.

"This is the one," Milos said with finality. He always knew exactly what he wanted.

"It is exquisite, no?" said the charming grey-haired owner, an immigrant from France who was a third-generation jeweler. Half the items in the store were new, his designs, and lovely. But, I still had my heart set on an antique ring.

"The price, is that the best you can do? We like a few other rings at other stores. This one is the best so far, but we are trying to decide," Milos said. He was bartering, which made me laugh. Lying through his teeth—there were no other rings in the running, but the owner was ready for this song and dance. A lot of the time, they expect you to negotiate on jewelry, especially at smaller establishments.

"Well, we are having a sale starting next week. You are in luck! Let me look up what the price on this is going to be. Hold on."

Shuffling his feet, the owner navigated back to his computer and typed away. Locating my potential engagement ring in his catalog, he was more than likely seeing what he had invested in it and the wiggle room. Poking his calculator, he reached a number as he again approached.

"For that ring, all in, tax included, you are looking at sixty-one thousand, six hundred and twenty-five dollars."

Our new Parisian friend explained how we had to put a percentage down if we wanted to hold it, and we could either make payments or fork out the full amount upon pickup. Milos smartly told him that he wanted to do some research and sleep on it.

I was giddy as we left the store, not because of the ring, but because this was actually happening.

A physical representation of commitment. Emotionally, we were back on track. Communicating again, making plans, working together. My guard was down, and I was letting him back in. Relationships are so complex and I was beginning to understand the work that it took to keep the spark going.

It was decided—that was going to be my engagement ring. In two weeks, Milos was going to buy it outright.

After rings came house shopping. My adorable bungalow was amazing, but it was about to get a bit crowded. There was literally no room for a crib anywhere, and all that is needed when bringing home an infant.

The latest ultrasound had confirmed it, we were going to have a little boy. Milos was thrilled. In Serbian culture, it is good luck to have a male first. They are extremely superstitious and believe that the eldest son is the protector of the family. Secretly, I was hoping for a girl, but regardless, I was starting to grow fond of the tiny parasite.

What was Milos's budget for a house? Five to fifteen million. My life was turning into an actual fairy tale.

Remember Maya, my realtor friend? She gladly agreed to start showing us high-end homes in Malibu, as we wanted to raise our son near the water, away from the pollution and close to good schools.

Barbara, my mom, made another trip out to check on us. Why not bring her along house hunting? The first place we looked at in Malibu was a five-acre property, complete with a teepee, greenhouse, tennis court, and mini colonial mansion. It belonged to a well-known movie star from the '70s. While the land was amazing, the house was an expensive mess. Each room had a different theme and had been remodeled as such. Weirdest part, it smelled. Wet dog stench followed us in every room and we quickly decided to pass.

The second house was heaven. A horse farm on four acres, with a water well and lush landscaping. You could tell that the home had been just that, home. Loved and enjoyed, the old two-story farm house was warm and inviting. High ceiling with crown molding and dark, wide plank wood flooring. The master on the second level was by far my favorite. Attached was an office that could easily be turned into a nursery, and a wide balcony lent us a view of the garden and the ocean in the distance.

Its price tag was a measly twelve million.

Literally, unfathomable.

Twelve million seems like nothing when you have billions of dollars; it is all relative. Milos was used to this kind of extravagance, but I was highly uncomfortable.

My love wasn't totally sold on Malibu. If he received a residency at UCLA, which was the closest teaching hospital, his commute each day would easily be two hours long. With his lengthy shifts and a strenuous career, it was looking more and more like we would end up in San Diego.

July 1, 2016

Taking a break from my hiatus on YouTube, I uploaded a video called "I'm Engaged and Pregnant." The internet went crazy. Goody-two-shoes Brittani was knocked up by a hella fine doctor and tying the knot. Milos's only request was that I tell everyone we met at Roasters, not on Tinder. His friends would never let him live it down if they found out he had selected his bride from a dating app.

That video launched my career into vlogging, video blogs about our life together. We were basically curating our own mini reality TV show. It was perfect because I was still dealing with morning sickness and wasn't able to work twelve-hour days. The vlogs were way easier to make, seemingly harmless.

Lui was the real star. That dog just seemed to know when the camera was on him, hamming it up for his adoring fans. Exotic rich foreigner meets quirky American, plus cute animal, equaled a hit. The views and subscribers kept climbing, week after week, as we gave them a glimpse into our romantic journey.

At the end of July, Maya hooked us up with Pat Smith, a realtor who specialized in homes in Rancho Santa Fe. If you are ever in San Diego, go, drive around, you will get it. Houses are crowded together in Beverly Hills and most of Los Angeles, while in Rancho Santa Fe it is the opposite. Sprawling estates and rolling hills. Wineries, ranches, and privacy, yet you are still close to civilization. No wonder Oprah, Bill Gates, and many of the crème de la crème choose to make it their primary dwelling.

My ob-gyn was now in San Diego as well. Milos was convinced the medical care was superior at UC San Diego, and who was I to argue with an actual expert.

We lumped one of my baby appointments in with home shopping and decided to stay the night. Lui loved his boarding facility, as they doted on him and spoiled him with treats and attention. Our adventure would only add to the weekly vlog, so we had nothing to lose.

Pat was actually short for Patricia. She was a handsome lesbian with the mouth of a sailor. Not your typical luxury real estate agent, as she was a fan of tattoos and bowties, but she was a sharp dresser in her blue suit. It was obvious why she was good at her job. Pat knew exactly who she was and could care less whether you accepted her or not.

Pat reminded me of Ruby from *Orange is The New Black*, she was a confident anomaly.

Doctor's appointment went smoothly. I was gaining weight and on track. I made it back to our hotel just in time to meet up with our tour guide. Pat was going to be our property chauffeur, shuttling us from one multi-million-dollar piece of earth to the next. She was waiting outside of our hotel in her new red Porsche Cayenne, so we climbed in and headed out.

Our hotel was in La Jolla, so it was a short drive to the first listing.

The bar was set pretty high, the ranch in Malibu still in the back of my mind, but it couldn't compare to the homes in Rancho Santa Fe.

Two were positively beyond anything of my wildest dreams. The first, a Spanish style compound. Eight-thousand-square-foot monster with a guest house, pool, and putting green. You know you are on the right track when you start picturing yourself living there, where you would place items you already own.

There was a tranquil spot for a playground, under a large shaded tree in a somewhat bare corner of grass. One of the guest houses would make an awesome game room, a place where our son could hang out with his friends and have movie nights.

It was special, but the last home we looked at that day was indescribable.

Also a Spanish style villa, there were four houses on the five-acre property. The main house, a guest house, another guest house with a gym on the bottom level, and a whole separate building that was just a movie theatre and for entertainment. Close enough together for convenience, yet spread far enough apart for aesthetics.

If we bought this particular property, I would never leave. I would live in the closet and master bath, which connected to a salt water pool with a waterfall. I would have barbeques, learn to cook, and watch my son play on the expansive grounds inside the massive stone walls that guarded its beauty.

New plan. Buy the property, have ten children, die happy.

Milos had me make a separate video so he could get Zora and Nikola onboard. It was his money, but they were back in Serbia and he understandably wanted to be able to share this moment with them. Of course, they both wholeheartedly agreed that it was worth every penny.

The owners were asking for eight million, we could probably get it for a little over seven, and it needed only slight remodeling to fit our needs.

We looked at the Spanish style abode one more time, driving there and back that same week just to make sure.

Milos and I were finally free from the curse that seemed to have clouded our relationship from the start.

Pat was super chill, aware that it might be a few more weeks before we could put in a solid offer. There had been some delays with Sven and Arthur. Getting the banks to communicate with their employees, who seemed to constantly be on holiday, was proving a challenge.

Cautiously, that Saturday, I uploaded the video in which we were looking at these pricey properties. I didn't want to alienate anyone, but I didn't want to hide my life anymore, either. It was done as casually as possible, not trying to rub it in anyone's face. Thankfully, our viewers were wholeheartedly supportive, and on the edge of their seats to see what we were going to choose.

Now that my second baby was on the way, it was time to let go of my first. My first home in Highland Park. Maya helped me market it and get it ready for sale. If it had just been Milos and I, you would have had to drag me out kicking and screaming. As a couple, we were trading up, but it broke my heart to part with it.

Being practical, it just didn't make sense to hold onto it. Let's say, when Milos got his money out, we paid it off and kept it. The neighborhood wasn't safe enough to have a child, the schools were the worst in the state, and the real estate market was volatile. What if I rented it out? I wouldn't be able to handle if it was trashed or mistreated by tenants. The best option was to sell.

Any day now, Milos would have his money...but I still had money troubles of my own.

Not working for four months and paying for absolutely everything had put me well over twenty thousand dollars in debt. Milos kept offering to chip in once he got his money, but I wanted to fix this on my own.

It took three weeks, but my lovely home was finally ready to be put on the MLS. A deck was installed, wood chips covering the bare dirt in the backyard. Fresh paint and clean windows. My quaint little haven was worth well over what I had paid for it.

To my dismay, it sold in the first week. A bidding war between two buyers pushed it to the point that all my debt would be cleared. I had basically lived there the past three years for free, including all the costs of upgrades and maintenance. Even now, it is painful to think about.

That home was my friend. I used to hug the walls at night when I woke up and needed to empty my bladder. It was the best listener, great for game nights, and the perfect backdrop to countless videos. It was going to be missed.

The countdown had started. I was seven months pregnant, moving, and overwhelmed.

With any sale comes inspections, which were made even more complicated by what happened next.

Milos had pushed his board exam until December 1. It was do or die. He was studying somewhere in the house while I slowly packed. My belly kept getting in the way of the boxes, but it felt good to have something to keep me in motion.

"Brittani, can we talk?" A troubled Milos stood at our dining room table while I wrapped paper around some of my delicate antiques.

"Something has happened. Nikola is on it, as is Sven, but Arthur has disappeared."

Thump, thump, my heart was beating with growing concern.

"Arthur has stolen the money and vanished. There is a paper trail, Nikola will find him, but it might take some time before everything is worked out."

I was speechless. What now? My house was sold. I was in debt and needed to clear the balance. YouTube had picked up and I could fully recover in another six months, but Maya had worked so hard and I couldn't back out at the last minute. It was too late.

Trying not to cry, as I could see Milos was crestfallen, I woman-ed up.

"Well, what should we do?" I asked, genuinely trying to come up with a solution.

"What do you want to do? I am so sorry. I feel like I have let you down."

Time to be smart. Milos would have his remaining two board exams done by the end of December at the latest. Our son would already be born, and Milos would easily be able to get a residency at one of the four hospitals in San Diego, earning more than enough each month to take care of us.

It would be harder, but I could work from anywhere.

"We stick to the plan. Let's look for an apartment, or a house in San Diego, and we will figure out the rest as we go."

I gave him a hug, hoping beyond hope that I was right.

Chapter 9

NESTING AND PORN

October 26, 2016

Moving day. We had stumbled upon a newly built complex of townhouses for rent. They were pricey, even more expensive than my mortgage, but Milos would have a job by the end of January. With my house selling, I had a small surplus of cash that should keep us comfortable until then.

It was three bedrooms, with a two-car garage, so thankfully none of my furniture would need to go into storage. Things would be tight, but temporary.

My due date was November 30, only a little over a month away and finally I was looking pregnant. Again, my poor mom. She drove back over to help me finish packing, so Milos could study, and then she would join us in San Diego to help us get settled.

Another good thing about the sale was that I could repay her. When my father had passed away, there was a decent amount of life insurance money. My mom had generously made the down payment, getting me out of the apartment life that had been my digs for the past ten years.

The rental office in San Diego for our new housing was only open until a certain time, so once the moving truck was loaded, Milos and Lui booked it down, leaving my mother and I to lock up and hide the keys for Maya.

It was weird, standing in the living room with everything gone.

The house echoed, sad as well from our parting. My chest throbbed. It felt wrong, I didn't want to be leaving, not like this. My life wasn't about me or what I wanted anymore. As a parent, you have to make sacrifices.

Tears were shed as I drove down to my new life. Thankfully, my mom had to operate her own vehicle, so she wouldn't have to witness me grieving. I let them flow freely down my face, washing away my past and getting myself ready for the next chapter.

The following few weeks were spent unpacking and making lists of things that we needed to get, sorting objects into piles to donate. I wasn't even close to having all the recommended items for a newborn, but God Bless Amazon.

Milos was barely sleeping, up until the wee hours of the morning studying. He pushed his USMLE Step One test for the very last time to December 30, wanting to go through his Pathology book that he already knew by heart. He was ready and I just wanted him to take the test for crying out loud, but I also tried to understand things from his point of view.

Higher test scores meant a better residency, which meant a happier Milos.

Feisty Maya threw me a baby shower, which we drove back up to LA to attend. It was simple but beautiful, most of the food being homemade and with my closest friends all in one place at the same time. We laughed, we played cliché party games, and we went home feeling extremely loved and spoiled, especially with the thoughtful gifts they had bestowed on us.

Before I forget, you probably want an update on Arthur. Well, Nikola's connections had located him hiding out in Greece.

Showing me on his laptop, Milos had an official letter from a Russian tycoon that was looking to convert rubles to euros. It was the perfect scheme for Arthur to launder a large portion of the money he had stolen. If he tried to spend it without converting it, it was traceable, which the retired banker was well aware of.

Sven was acting as a double agent of sorts, brokering what Arthur thought was a deal behind Nikola's back.

Part of the arrangement was that Arthur would have to meet the tycoon and his banker at a specific date and specific time.

"What happens if Arthur does show up? To this fake meeting?"

Smirking, Milos flashed me a devious look.

"You don't want to know."

Suddenly, I was really grateful that we didn't get any of the money. Not like this.

"Milos, if the plan works, I don't want any of it. Can you just be a doctor and I will make silly videos and we will live happily ever after?"

His face, tan from his study sessions at the pool, was getting even more freckles. The ends of his eyelashes were bleached as well. Hug, kiss, he nodded his head and we snuggled up to watch something online, trying to forget Arthur and his probable demise.

Nesting. It is real. The closer we got to my due date, me, nesting maniac. Everything had to be in its place. Crib was delivered, bottles and anything that might come close to the baby's mouth were sterilized. Milos kept trying to get me to slow down, but my ob-gyn said, "Do whatever feels natural, as long as you don't lift anything heavy."

My car was suddenly not safe, and Milos's? Nope, it had to go. The old BMW was suffering, put it out of its misery. Trade it in and move on.

That is exactly what we did. Traded in my car for a new, very safe large SUV and Milos's car for a sedan. Mercedes was having an insane special, with payments close to what I was currently covering on the cars we already owned.

Milos's enthusiasm for San Diego was starting to rub off on me. We took walks on the beach when we could, slow because of my belly and limited lung capacity. He pointed out constantly how much cleaner the city was, how everyone was more educated and friendly.

Personally, I thought they were all overly talkative because of Prozac, but still.

My mom's plan was to come, help us move, go back to Arizona, and then come back to San Diego a few days before my due date. Trouble was, every doctor's appointment they kept pondering how low the baby was sitting and fully expected me to go into labor at any moment.

She just stayed, waiting for me to pop out a human.

A last-minute job through my management had come in for a bakery, and the pay was pretty decent! My proposal was a short, thirty-second stop motion animation about my nesting woes, and the brand loved the concept.

Being the resourceful gal that I am, I found a small green screen studio thirty minutes away that was ready to go. All I needed to do was bring my camera, round belly, and fiancé with me.

November 18, 2016

We loaded up the car and headed to Carlsbad, filmed a very fun and goofy video for a few hours, and then made our way straight back to the townhouse. I had yet another deadline, having to edit that afternoon to get the footage to my friend who does animation. He would need to work on it all night and have it back to me by the following morning, with added effects and pizzazz, so I could send it to the brand.

But it didn't help that Milos was being grumpy. He picked a fight at the green screen studio, in front of my mom. I didn't want to throw out the garlic bread from the video on their sound stage, as it would quickly stink up the building. Having been on a set or two, I knew it was bad manners to leave strong smelling food on a hot set (a set that was in-use), especially when it wasn't a part of their production.

I didn't want to be known as the pregnant girl that left garlic bread to permeate their space, forcing them to buy air freshener and open all their doors in hopes of vacating the stench.

What did Milos do? Grabbed the garlic bread tray out of my hands as we were leaving, marched right back in, and threw it in the very trash I had been trying to avoid.

Told you, stupid fight.

My mom was irritated, as was I, but I didn't want her in the middle of any of our issues. Maybe if Milos just went and played tennis, he would calm down and come to his senses.

Back at the townhouse, I was editing away on my computer, Milos was off smacking fuzzy green objects with a small racket, and I was praying to go into labor and be able to see my toes again.

My mom gasped.

You see, Milos had loaned my mom his laptop. We didn't have cable, my desktop computer was in for repair, and I was editing on my laptop. She could either read one of my teen sci-fi fantasy novels or browse articles about gardening online.

Opening up a web browser, she went to type "YouTube" into the address bar and it started populating previously viewed suggested sites. YouJizz. YouPorn.

"Brittani, is this what I think it is?" she said, her mouth hanging wide open.

As quick as an eight-month-soon-to-be-nine pregnant woman can be, I was up and taking the laptop from her, turning it towards myself to see what had her flustered.

Thump, thump, thump, my heart sped up.

I like to think I know my way around computers, enough to go into Milos's history. The last few days were clean, nothing interesting. Just Serbian news sites, medical blogs, and links to his online practice exams.

But you can also search for key words in someone's history. Wild guess, but I typed in "sex" and was flooded with page after page of results. It wasn't just porn; a lot of it was interactive, live, seriously kinky.

Looking at the dates next to the links, he had been watching this crap almost every night. When he was supposedly studying. He was studying all right, just not the subject or subjects I had expected.

God, I was getting so sick of my heart being broken.

I took a couple of screenshots of his browsing history, and I emailed them to myself. Contemplated making them his desktop background and screensaver and gauging his reaction when he got home.

I was hurt and furious. There is something sacred about pregnancy. I was carrying his child; it is a time for a woman to be worshiped and adored, not this. Not waiting to confront him in person, heated words were exchanged on the phone.

His excuse was lackluster. Blah blah blah, he didn't want to pester me too much for sex in my "condition," so he had sought alternative means to relieve his stress, blah.

And the timing was perfect. My mom now hated Milos, Zora was flying in literally days to be there for the birth, and my fiancé was binge-watching threesomes and flirting with web cam girls.

Real life isn't like a movie, it's hard and unpredictable and weird. It doesn't, and never will, make sense.

Milos came home from tennis with flowers, completely embarrassed and appalled that his future mother-in-law also knew his dirty little secret. Hours spent online researching porn addiction and others in similar situations helped me cope, realizing that our predicament wasn't exactly unique.

All I wanted was for it to go away. I had worked too hard and come too far and I was determined to have a beautiful birth and bring my son into an environment of love. Later, I would deal with my true feelings.

That is not what I needed. Talk about a bumpy few days. Many hours of chatting finally smoothed things over enough that when Zora arrived on November 27, Mom and Milos had called a cease-fire.

Both of them loved me, and I wanted peace.

Milos went to pick up Zora from LAX, as the flights to San Diego International Airport from Serbia take longer. Thinking it a kind gesture, my mom and I had gone shopping and picked up a bathrobe, slippers, and some magazines to make Zora feel welcome.

Barbara, Milos, Zora, a new baby, Lui, and myself were all going to be in the same apartment together, possibly for months.

Here goes nothing.

Meeting us at a popular restaurant, the first thing Zora said to me was, "Where is my grandson?" before giving me a big hug and a smooch on my cheek. Trust me, I was wondering the same thing.

"On the laptop in my womb, he has pay-per-view! Just like Daddy!"

Point Brittani.

Zora was chattering away in broken English, excited to finally be in the thick of the action and not on the other end of a phone call begging for details.

While pregnant, you have to write in a chart your kick counts. Preferably at night, or when the baby is most active, making sure that you get a certain amount of kicks in a certain amount of time.

Well, the little sucker hadn't moved all day, and it was starting to worry me.

Welcome to America, Zora, but we are going to go to the hospital now. My doctor had been very intent: If you don't get your kick counts, come in right away.

No sooner did they have the monitors around my swollen belly than the little stinker started kicking, and furiously. My tummy was a drum, and he was way off rhythm. The on-call resident sent us home after twenty minutes, assuring us that all was normal.

December 4, 2016
In the middle of the night, I went into false labor. Everyone was up, dressed, timing my contractions at one in the morning and then they slowed down and stopped. Seriously?

December 5, 2016
Finally, around 4:30 a.m., my water broke.

Milos was calm, his medical training kicking in. Zora and my mom were excitedly hovering, making sure I had my overnight bag and a towel. Correction—multiple towels, because my body would not stop leaking fluid.

It was go time.

Chapter 10

OUR SON

Absolutely nothing was going to ruin my day of birth. And I mean, quite literally, almost a full day of labor.

Twenty-three hours, to be exact.

You should have seen me at the hospital, making laps around the nurse's station while hooked up to a monitor, trying to get my contractions closer together. I was cracking jokes, dancing, overjoyed to finally meet my little creation.

My hospital gown was extra stylish, with the open back and my large underwear that was absorbing the liquid from my amniotic sack on full display.

I looked hot.

Milos had only gotten maybe two hours' sleep before I went into labor, as he was supposedly up studying. Not even his mental infidelity was going to spoil my mood.

A few hours in, Zora and Milos had passed out on the large couch in my luxury birthing suite. The new wing of the hospital had opened two weeks prior. It felt more like a high-end hotel than a hospital. As impressive as it was, the establishment was organized chaos, with most of the staff being temporary until they filled all the permanent positions.

I really wanted to have a natural birth. Call me crazy, but I wanted to end with a bang. Nothing about my pregnancy had been easy, so why stop now.

Here's the rub. Twelve hours in and I wasn't dilated enough, plus my contractions were slowing down. Because my water had broken first, which was unusual, there was a greater risk of infection. The nurses decided to hook me up with a drip, and start administering Pitocin.

Some midwives have mentioned to me since that women can go days after their water breaks before giving birth. All I had at the time was the advice of my doctor and the doctors at the hospital. Not an expert on this, so don't quote me. My situation might have been more complex than that, as it was dubbed a high-risk pregnancy on my insurance pay outs, so whatevs.

Hour twelve to hour fifteen were by far the worst. The drugs quickly ramped up my contractions at an unnatural rate. They went from level four, five on the pain scale, to level ten. Each spasm of my uterus was excruciating.

It didn't help that Milos was watching movies, one of them being *Angry Birds*, glued to his phone while I was starving and pushing out a human. Zora, as well, was behaving oddly. Not as sweet as I had remembered her, more intense. She sat, silently sipping coffee and staring at me as the cycles of pain came and went.

I repeat, nothing was going to ruin this.

When the resident checked my pelvis at hour fifteen and stated that I was progressing nicely, only five or six more hours to go, I changed my mind about the whole natural birth thing.

Drugs, give me drugs.

The first epidural numbed only half my body, which was hysterical. It wasn't that funny, but I like dealing with my fear in humor. Second epidural did the trick. At hour seventeen, because it was a busy night and it took a while to get an anesthesiologist to my room, I finally had relief.

All I wanted to do was sleep or eat a grilled cheese.

Maybe grilled cheese, then sleep, but no luck.

They don't let you eat while in labor except for very small, controlled amounts. If there were any complications and you had to have a C-section, you couldn't have a loaded down stomach.

I tried to rest my eyes, but the annoying cuff measuring my blood pressure beeped and squeezed my left arm on a regular interval, making sleep impossible.

Finally, it was time to push.

December 6, 2016

Zora and my mom exited, leaving Milos, the nurse, and me to the task at hand.

Milos was relaxed, keeping a close eye on things, which was reassuring. Part of his medical school training had been three weeks spent in labor and delivery. He knew what was coming and what to look out for.

By that point, pushing was the easy part. I was numb, giddy, and ready. Some hipster song was rolling out of the fancy speaker system installed in the room. Everyone got to talking. I explained to our hospital audience how Milos and I had met and how I had avoided his advances for months. They ate it up as we chatted away. So much so that the medical resident, staff doctor, and nurse had to be reminded when a contraction was coming so they could guide me through it.

"Do you want to deliver your son?" inquired the resident doctor, smiling at Milos.

She was Korean, with simple no-nonsense glasses and her hair pulled back in a ponytail. Willowy and tall, easily over six feet. I don't remember her name, but she was a fourth-year resident and extremely sharp. I felt comfortable that she was at the helm of my birthing ship.

Only a few more pushes and it would all be over.

"Yes, sure, of course." Milos was suddenly nervous.

It was probably a bit different being a doctor to your own child versus a perfect stranger.

Heading over to a drawer in a cabinet close by, the nurse inquired over her shoulder, "What is your glove size?"

Pause. I could tell that Milos was overwhelmed.

"Don't worry, I think you're a medium. Try these."

Handing him the white rubber gloves, the nurse was right back at my side, letting the resident doctor and her supervisor do the heavy lifting.

One last push and our son was out. Milos was holding a wrinkly little body. The doctors helped him place the tiny angel on my bare chest.

What was the first thing that I said?

Tears streaming down my tired cheeks as I held my precious, precious baby boy.

"I want more!"

Laughter erupted. Apparently, that is not a normal reaction.

Looking over at my Milos, awe and wonder filled his features. Unshed emotion pooled at the corners of his eyes.

I scooted over so he could partially lay on the gurney and be next to us. In that moment, the doctors and nurse were forgotten, there was no one else in the room but us three.

I couldn't stop crying and staring and kissing Milos, and our baby, gently rubbing his tiny little head.

"He smells like Dr. Pepper," Milos stated, getting an even bigger laugh.

My heart was swollen with a love greater than I could have ever imagined. Afraid to blink, as I might miss some tiny detail, I stared at our beautiful child. His wet brown hair was curly and covered his head, with ridiculously long eyelashes sprouting out of his large, dark eyes. A cute little button nose hovered above a set of red, full lips.

The dimple in his chin was identical to my own, something I had inherited from my father.

He was perfect.

The little guy didn't cry, just kept making the same noise over and over. "OOO, ooo, ooo, OOO, ooo, OOO." Looking around the room, it was like he was saying, "What the heck just happened!"

It didn't take long for him to quiet down. Our little boy knew he was with his momma as he snuggled my chest, melting to the sound of my heartbeat.

Too infatuated with my mini-miracle, I hardly noticed the doctors furiously working to put me back together. I had several tears that they had to hop on fast before I lost too much blood.

It was the best day of my life.

We didn't rush bringing our parents back into the room. Hours went by with just Milos, Misha, and I. We chose Misha because it was the name of Milos's late grandfather. Milos described him as a kind, hardworking man who would have done anything for his family.

My baby daddy also wanted his son to have a Serbian name, understandably, and I didn't care what he was called as long as he was mine.

Little Misha was six pounds, eighteen ounces and almost twenty-three inches long. He was skinny, but strong, able to lift his head up and turn it side-to-side while on his stomach at not even a day old. My long labor, however, had left him with a tight jaw and stiff neck, so getting him to breastfeed was another story.

Feeling that we couldn't keep the rest of the gang waiting in suspense any longer, it was time to bring in the grandmas. Our nurse was attempting to get my little man to latch as they entered, to no avail. He was fussing, hungry and wanting his first breakfast. Before baby, I would have been mortified to have my boobs out on display in front of my mother and almost mother.

After baby, no shits given.

All I cared about was my son and his needs. I would have run around fully naked at the hospital if that is what it would have taken to fill his belly.

Seeing my mom's face as she entered and spotted Misha for the first time was adorable. Clapping her hands together, she cooed and fawned, exclaiming that he was the most beautiful thing she had ever seen, and introduced herself as one of his grandmothers.

Zora was a different story.

Seeing me struggle with getting him to feed, trying different positions, she marched up to the bed, grabbed my right breast, and tried to push Misha's head to the position she thought was correct.

I grabbed her hand, shoved it away, and drew my baby away from her reach.

My reaction was instant and swift; all my instincts were on overdrive and they screamed, "Keep Zora away from your son!"

Furious, she marched out of the room, and returned a few minutes later.

Oh no. I had not seen this coming.

Chapter 11

GRAM-MONSTER

If you're pregnant, and reading my story, get as much rest as possible before you birth because the first three days are the hardest.

Not mentally challenging as much as physically taxing.

We were moved from the birthing suite to a recovery room where they would monitor my healing, perform multiple tests on our new offspring, and make sure we had a hang of things before sending us off on our merry way.

Misha was such a sweet newborn. Relaxed and easygoing, barely grunting when they drew his blood and administered some of his first shots. Crying was too much work unless he was hungry.

The nurses kept saying, "Just wait, he's tired from the birth. Give it twenty-four hours."

Wrong. A full day came and went and he was still the same. My conclusion was that Misha was either really smart and already had everything figured out, or not-so-bright and oblivious. Either way, I loved him to pieces.

Milos and Zora had headed back to our apartment shortly after our transition, as Lui needed to be let out and cared for. They were also going to get some rest and return later that afternoon.

Partially what prompted their hasty exit was Zora's continued behavioral issues.

Let me set the scene. Our cozy new room was a twin to the previous, just on a smaller scale and on a different floor. After getting changed into a new hospital gown, my heart was full, but my stomach was painfully empty. I would have eaten cardboard at that point if it would have dulled the hunger pains.

The hospital had a menu, room service style, so we called and eagerly put in our orders.

Less than thirty minutes later, a sweet young man with red hair knocked on our open door and then wheeled in a cart loaded with our meals before shyly making his exit. My mom jumped up to divvy out our specific orders, knowing that I was absolutely famished. Eggs, toast, oatmeal, and fruit for me. An omelet and toast for Milos, you get the idea.

As she went to hand my fiancé his tray, Zora popped up so that she was in between them and yanked it out of her hands.

"I feed my son!" she said. Glaring, she turned and handed the tray to Milos.

He acted as if nothing had happened, lifting off the top lid and inspecting the contents. My mom stood there, stunned.

I chalked all of it up to lack of sleep and stress. Maybe Zora was testy because of the time change, traveling, feeling left out, language issues, a myriad of excuses.

Her behavior was uncalled for as I was working through my own issues at the moment. Selfish, as she was aware that I had bigger problems, like feeding my child. Four different lactation consultants confirmed that breastfeeding was pretty much a lost cause, which was incredibly frustrating.

Everything after that was a blur.

Awake for almost thirty hours, using a breast pump every hour so I could carefully transfer colostrum to a feeding syringe and patiently get every drop I could into my baby...talk about a rough start. My "nothing is going to ruin this" attitude was still holding, even poked and prodded and bone weary.

It is the same now as it was then. When it comes to taking care of my son, I don't hesitate.

I spent two days in the hospital after the birth. Misha finally could kind of latch; it took him forever to eat, but the experts were satisfied enough to give us the boot. From there on out, we were on our own.

It was hysterical putting Misha in his take-home outfit that he was positively swimming in. I had failed to purchase any newborn clothing, only zero to three months and above, convinced that my child couldn't possibly ever be that tiny. Luckily, there was a boutique with kid items next to our townhouse. One of the first stops would be to correct my error in fabric judgment.

Feeling nostalgic, I packed every baby hat and swaddle blanket the hospital had provided. Not technically stealing, as all the items on the cart were paid for by insurance, which would eventually be partially paid by me. Speaking of swaddling, Misha was impossible. No matter how tightly you had him wrapped, his hands were out in under a minute.

He was a baby Houdini and already making me laugh.

Normally when I am in a car, as a driver or passenger, I am relatively relaxed. With Misha, every vehicle I spotted was the enemy. Adding to my mental list that I needed to purchase a "Baby On Board" window sign so the world would understand that we were carrying precious cargo.

Sitting next to Misha in the middle row, I was endlessly checking to see if the car seat straps were too tight or if he was warm enough.

Not a peep. The nugget just chilled like he had done this a million times, his dark eyes open and his breathing wheezy from his still developing lungs.

As much as I was ready to leave the hospital, I was dreading being in the townhouse with the current climate.

Three bedrooms, two bathrooms, totaling 1,300 square feet: it wasn't the biggest space for now four humans and a large dog.

Privacy was non-existent.

We had a celebratory dinner our first night. Zora had made salmon, potato soup with buckwheat, as well as roasted vegetables on the side. That woman could cook. Milos had purchased a thoughtful card with an even sweeter hand-written message. What you would expect in a love note, the pouring of one's heart to paper.

I really did have hope. Hope that we could all be in one living space and get along.

Sadly, Zora was just getting started.

After a beautiful dinner, in which I kept leaking breast milk through my shirt and had surrendered to stuffing hand towels into my nursing bra, it was time for Misha to get his first sponge bath. Having done my research, I had bought a special tub that would suspend our son like a hammock so his umbilical cord wouldn't be affected.

Sorry about the reference to my leaking coconuts, but when I set out to tell this story, I promised myself that I would be honest to a fault even if it was uncomfortable.

Cheers to awkward moments.

Zora insisted that we put chamomile tea bags in with the water to steep before using. I Google, discover it's fine, why not. Producing a pink round container of lotion from the depths of her suitcase, Zora swears that it is "the best" thing to use on a new baby. My soon-to-be-husband agreed that it would be superior to what I had purchased.

None of this bothered me. Misha wasn't just my son, he was Milos's son, and it was only fair that he had some say in his care.

What royally pissed me off was that Zora didn't even wait to ask if I wanted help in the bathing process before diving in and giving our first born his first bath.

"You wash from here to face, and hold like this, see?" she said.

Every article I had read stated, in bathing, you go from the cleanest to the dirtiest. Why would you clean their cute little butts and then proceed to use the same towel and water on their sensitive faces? I mean hello! Logic!

Working quickly, she flipped him in her arms so he was facing down. With his neck in one of her hands, scrubbing his back with the other, and in general giving me a heart attack. Misha's pink arms and legs were flailing.

Feeling my temper rising, I was irate.

I should be having this first moment with our son. I wanted to be gentle and go slow.

Leaning over to me, concerned, my mom whispered in my ear, "Your chest, are you alright?"

Red patches were blossoming from my new-found cleavage up. A physical manifestation of my current stress levels.

Not that Zora noticed.

Misha was cleaned, slobbered with the sweet-smelling contents of the pink jar, and Zora carried him to our bed to put on a diaper. Not once asking if I wanted to be handling these responsibilities. My hands felt tied, trying not to be rude by pointing out her rudeness.

Feigning exhaustion, I shooed everyone out of our bedroom but Milos, our now almond-scented offspring, and myself.

Misha was out in under five minutes, having found the experience as draining as I did.

"My mother wants to give you her necklace. You know, the one I showed you? With the diamonds?"

Months before, Milos had called me over while on his laptop to show me a picture of the jewelry piece. He had explained that Zora wanted it to go to whoever Milos married. It was hard to describe, loop after loop of metal created a flowing ring of gold and diamonds that would drape around one's neck like a collar.

I could have sworn that Zora was listening at the door; I saw shadows of tiny feet through the crack at the base.

"Would Barbara come back to Serbia with me? I'm thinking, next week? We could do a really quick trip. Just fly there, get it, bring it back. Having an American citizen carrying it, she won't be questioned. I really want you to have it."

According to Milos, Nikola and himself had bought if for Zora as a surprise.

Also, according to Milos, the necklace was valued at over two hundred fifty thousand dollars. Southwest turquoise rings were more my speed, but it was a sweet gesture.

"I don't think she will go, but that is very kind of you to offer!" I placated, already knowing what her answer would be. I still brought it up to Barbara the following morning. Not even having the full request pass through my lips before she was shaking her head in refusal.

"There is no way I am leaving you," she said.

And thank God she didn't.

In Zora's eyes, nothing I did was good enough.

Diapers? I kept putting them on wrong, as she examined and adjusted my work after every changing.

"We need to bind his hips, it is good."

She was a broken record. It didn't matter that every pediatrician at the hospital, plus his new primary doctor, stated that it was unnecessary and barbaric.

My son's belly button was slightly protruding, a totally normal occurrence in the healing process. Whether he had an innie or an outie didn't matter to me. Zora's repeated suggestion was to place a coin and secure it with gauze wrapped around his stomach, forcing it down.

Another thing his new pediatrician was firmly against.

How I burped him? Wrong. Chalking it up to my inexperience because it took me longer than she thought it should.

My lack of singing? Wrong. I should be singing to him.

His clothes? Or lack thereof? Appalling.

My little tyke was a heater. Even in the womb, I would only sleep with a sheet on at night because I had my own personal bed warmer. During his gestation, you could have spotted me at Whole Foods on a daily basis just standing in the freezer section, my eyes closed in blissful relief.

Wearing any of the newborn clothing we tried, even when the material was paper thin and purely cotton, Misha would start sweating and fussing. My mommy instincts said no clothes, just a diaper, and swaddled in a cotton muslin blanket that was breathable, was the way to go.

No different than his first few days at the hospital.

Zora kept insisting that he needed to wear a onesie.

"Brittani, he is baby. He is cold. Touch, see? He needs clothes. What are you doing?"

Followed by her clucking and shaking her head, taking Misha from my arms.

You do not, I repeat, do not take a brand-new baby from a mother without her offering.

Day by day, the situation declined.

"We need to get Misha Serbian citizenship," Zora exclaimed. Not a question.

"Of course, Mama, when we get the birth certificate, we will apply for it," Milos told her.

How had I not noticed before that Milos was a Mama's boy? Maybe I had been too in love to realize, and desperately wanting Zora's approval, I had overlooked her bossy nature.

Serbian citizenship? This set off warning bells in my head. What if Milos and I were in Serbia, with Misha, and Milos decided that he wanted to stay? What then, when our son was also a citizen, but I was not?

Worry. Worry prevented me from sleeping, up constantly with anxiety and struggling to breastfeed. Thankfully, I had Milos explain to Zora that when I was feeding her grandbaby, I wanted privacy as my boobs were constantly on full display. The perfect excuse for her to leave me alone for small periods of time.

I kept waiting for Milos to take a strong interest in his son. He was detached, which was also un-expected. In my head, I had pictured him as a doting, loving father who would be taking a million photos and sitting by the hour, admiring what we had created.

My future physician needed to study for his boards, so he couldn't help me out at all with Misha. One nappy change and he had retired from diaper duty.

Milos decided the first night we returned to no longer sleep in our bedroom. His excuse was also his looming board exams, which he said he needed rest for to be able to cram in information. My mom and Zora offered to take over at night with Misha, giving me a break, but I didn't trust Zora and it wouldn't be fair to ask that only my mother watched him.

Milos had to sleep somewhere, if not with us, so his solution was his mother's bedroom, to her odd delight. The more I kept her away from her grandson, the more Zora tried to keep Milos away from me.

Walking the hallways in the morning with Misha became a norm, as it provided a temporary escape from our prison.

I would peek my head into Zora's room to say hello, missing Milos terribly, but trying to understand. Shouldn't having a baby bring us closer together? It seemed to be creating a void in our relationship which I had no clue how to fix.

Vividly artificial red hair always caught my eye first. Zora sitting on her bed in one of her short nightgowns with Milos beside her on his laptop. Taking yet another practice quiz. She was reading one of the books I had loaned her and rubbing Milos's leg.

Zora was sans bra, or underwear, her large heavy cha-chas at full attention.

Their relationship was too close for comfort.

Where Zora was manipulative, my mom was a gift from heaven. She never pushed me to hold Misha, only waited for when I asked. She didn't tell me what to do or how to do it, but provided insight when requested. Without her steadiness, I would have cracked.

It was becoming plainly obvious that Zora was possessive. Milos was hers, and Misha was hers, period. The mind games extended to my mom as well, snippy remarks and sour looks.

Even crazier is that all of this happened in three days. Can you believe it? Three days, and lines had been drawn in the sand.

Where was the strong, but kind Zora I had first met? Who was this intruder in my home?

December 10, 2016

I had given up trying to breastfeed and was now pumping and feeding, which Misha was more than okay with. It would mean a lot more work on my end, with bottles and sterilizing parts, but he was fat and happy and loving the sudden steady flow of nutrients with minimal effort on his part. Hearing me talking to Misha, as he was still awake but milk drunk, Milos opened our bedroom door and popped his head in.

"How is he?" he inquired, still in his pajamas. He looked gorgeous in his white t-shirt and flannel pants. Even the scruff on his face added to his appeal.

"Perfect! Want to hold him?"

Please say yes. Please, please say yes! They had emphasized at the hospital that both parents should spend time each day with skin-to-skin contact. Bonding. Milos had only held Misha on his chest once, at the hospital, and that was it.

"Maybe in a bit. Can we talk?"

Yuck. My three least favorite words put together in that order to form a sentence. Can. We. Talk.

"Sure, come on in."

I lay Misha on the middle of the bed, so Milos could sit on the other side and kiss him or play with him if he so desired.

"Momma is upset. She says that you haven't been letting her hold Misha, but Barbara gets to hold him all the time. She flew all this way, Brittani, from another country, to be here for the birth."

Great, now I was being guilted.

Not wanting to add further strain, I picked our son back up and offered him to his father.

"She needs to understand that I am just more comfortable with my mom. And my mom is only really getting extra time while I am in the shower, but when, besides that, has it been unbalanced?"

Zora, stirring the pot for no reason.

"I know, but you always hand Misha to your mom when you go to grab things, but not to her."

Milos was now holding Misha, but it looked more like an obligation than a father cradling his son.

I gritted my teeth, frustrated.

"Milos, I have crazy protective instincts right now. Your parental unit doesn't listen! I leave her with Misha for one second and she is trying to put clothes on him. I have already told her no. Diaper and swaddle only. Or she keeps forcing the bottle on him when he is full, waking him up over and over to try to get him to eat more. And why?"

Our son was happy and healthy and well cared for. Frustrated, but wanting a resolution, I tried to come up with a compromise.

"How about you take him right now, and you and Zora spend time with him, alone. Then you can try to explain to Zora, gently, what is bothering me. Sound good?" I said.

He nodded his head, still holding Misha in his strong arms. Our little man had fallen asleep during our discussion and looked peacefully nestled in his embrace. I hated that he was being moved, but newborns aren't super sensitive to noise or being jostled around, so I let it go.

As Milos left the room, taking our son to Zora, I heard her squeal in glee and talk in a rapid baby voice in Serbian.

I wanted to tell her to shut up: whisper, you cow! Can't you see he is resting?

Post-partum hormone drop, as well as lack of sleep, was making me grumpy. Pondering our adventure into parenthood so far, it was grim. Not once had Milos opened his mouth and defended me when Zora opened hers and attacked.

So far, Zora hadn't offered to pay for a single thing, either. Not diapers, or the food we were eating, or even to foot part of the rent, which was my sole responsibility. Her son was set to inherit millions from her estate, and she couldn't even fork out a few dollars for a dinner here and there?

Milos offered to pay, with a debit card linked to my checking account, which meant that I still paid. So generous of him!

Lost, that is what I felt. At a loss. If it had been under a week and things were already horrid, how was I going to make it three more months? Milos had hinted she might stay even longer, closer to six.

My chest tightened. All I wanted was my son back. I didn't want him out of my sight.

The sound of knuckles tapping our closed bedroom room startled me from my thoughts.

"Come in!" I called.

Barbara entered, the sounds of Zora's cooing and Milos's rapid Serbian louder now.

"Good morning, did you sleep well?" I was smiling through the pain, but my mom was on to me.

"What's wrong now?" she said.

Closing the door behind her, I explained Zora's complaints. Shaking her head, I could tell that my mother was hurting for me and equally frustrated with how things were escalating.

Unnecessarily so.

"Honey, your chest. This isn't good for your health."

Red patches once again blanketed my chest and neck. Don't cry, don't cry, crap, crying.

"This is absolutely ridiculous. It isn't a competition! We should be doing everything to help you, not making it harder. Want me to go get Misha?"

This was my battle to fight. I quickly wiped my tears and stood up.

"I can get him! Hold on."

Grabbing my fuzzy grey bathrobe, I tied it in a loose knot and headed towards their voices.

Zora's door was open, and she and Milos were on either side of Misha, who was sandwiched in the middle.

I could have killed the bitch.

She had put two, thick blankets and a comforter over the top of Misha, leaving his head exposed. He was sweating and fussy, trying to get out from underneath the mountain of textiles. The little hair he had was in ringlets, curly and wet from exertion.

They were smiling and joking, Zora's arm wrapped possessively around Misha, giving me a smug look as she noticed me in the doorway. As if to say, "See, this is how it is done."

"Look at him, he is flawless. No marks," she said, rubbing his damp, struggling head with her thick fingers.

That. Was. It.

"Zora, what are you doing? He is miserable!" I snapped. Without pause, I walked the five feet to the bed, reached between them, gently picked up Misha, and left.

Milos would have started screaming at me if my mom hadn't still been in the room when I returned to the master suite. He was following close behind, fire in his eyes, and I could tell we would be having another lovely chat later.

I didn't care.

Gram Monster. Monster-in-Law. Evil troll. I called her every name in the book in my head, and more, as I hid the rest of the day in my bedroom with Misha. Not that Zora didn't knock on the door, at least once at hour.

"How is my baby?" she asked. Over. And over. And over.

Last time I checked, you didn't just give birth.

If he "belonged" to anyone, it would be Milos and me, and even then, Misha belonged to himself. He wasn't a possession, he was my heart.

Sure enough, Milos came to have a "talk" and take a break from "studying" around 7:00 p.m. that evening.

A rant was coming, but I wasn't having it.

"What is wrong with you?" he started.

"Wrong? Milos, did you not see our son, covered in sweat and straining to get out from under the blankets? Are you blind?"

Milos went to retort, but I cut him off.

"You just let her belittle me. You don't stand up to her! I am paying all the bills. Do I even have an engagement ring? No. I don't care if it costs ten dollars, you need to step up. Have you passed your board exams and gotten a job? No. It has been over a year when it should have been two months, as you promised. I am sick of everything being on me!"

I could tell I had struck a nerve, but it was the truth.

"You know that I have been trying to get the boards done. I took care of you all during your pregnancy!" Milos defended.

"I was lying in bed for five months, not moving. You have no excuse. There are no excuses, not anymore."

Milos softened. He knew that I was right, even if my verbal delivery was harsh.

"Do you want to go for a walk? With Misha?"

Getting out of the house sounded heavenly. It was a warm night and I had been wanting to try out my new baby carrier.

As luck had it, Misha was stirring. He was fed, changed, clothed, placed in the carrier with the newborn insert, and then draped with a swaddle blanket around him for good measure. We were ready for his first walk around the block.

Barbara had been trying to make an effort with Zora, hoping it would ease friction and maybe get her to back off.

Our respective creators were sitting in my mom's room, with Barbara on her bed and Zora on the computer chair. Her social media profile was pulled up, displaying pictures of her summer home in Bosnia.

"We are going for a walk!" I announced. Misha was already fast asleep in the odd contraption.

"Good for you guys! Where are you going to?" asked my mom, genuine.

"It is too cold out. Misha could get sick," Zora complained. "And my grandson could fall out, it is not safe."

Thanks for the buzzkill, not that I didn't expect it.

Pretending like I didn't hear a word she said, I smiled and retorted, "Be back in an hour! I have my phone if you guys need me!"

We walked the short five-minute path to the somewhat empty clubhouse and sat down on one of the outside couches by the pool. It was magical, with a fake fire pit in front of us, giving the night a soft glow. Far enough away to be safe and still warmed by the artificial heat.

"I had everything when I met you," Milos whispered, more to himself than for my ears.

It was the same discussion we'd had hundreds of times before—how he had had the world at his fingertips and gave it all up to be with me. I pretended to listen, but zoned out. I was enjoying the fresh air and time alone with my new family.

An hour went by and I was starting to fade. Relaxing for the first time in days, my eyes kept closing, begging me to let them stay shut and slumber.

We lazily wandered back to the townhouse. Milos was in a better mood after getting to talk about himself for an extended period of time.

Lui greeted us at the top of the stairs, shaking his butt in happiness upon our return. He had been such a good dog around his new friend, sniffing Misha and licking him a few times, but we were being extra cautious with their interactions until Misha was a little bit older and stronger.

That dog was a bowling ball, not always aware of his size, and had a tendency just to knock right into you when in play mode. Which was always.

Milos went to the kitchen to make an espresso as I headed to my mom's room with Misha still in my pack. I could tell when I entered the room, something had happened.

"Are you okay?" I asked.

"For the past hour, Zora has been off the rails. Texting and calling Milos, but he wasn't answering. Pacing, she kept saying that Misha is going to get sick. I tried to assure her that you guys were together and fine," my mom answered.

Milos's phone was on silent and he had left it at the apartment by accident.

Enough was enough. I blew.

Marching into the kitchen, where Zora was pouting on the couch, whining and lecturing Milos on the dangers of our outing, I confronted her in a heated whisper so as to not disturb Misha with this bullshit.

"Zora, can I talk to you? Alone?" I asked.

"Why? She can't understand, I have to translate," Milos interrupted.

Bull, fucking, shit. That woman understood every word I said, often feigning ignorance. I had caught her a few times in this, so I knew it to be true.

"I need to talk to Zora, now," I insisted.

"Anything that you have to say, you are going to have to say it in front of both of us! She can't understand!"

"Fine. Zora, I need you to back off. All I have wanted is your approval! I am a new mom! Is it so hard to just tell me that I am doing a good job?"

Laughing, Zora clucked her tongue, dismissing my statements.

"Brittani, what are you saying? I love you!" she replied.

It was like talking to a brick wall. I wanted to scream. I wanted to rip out my hair. Instead, I turned and left the living room and headed back to my mom's.

Milos and Zora were close behind. Barbara's sleeping quarters suddenly felt too small. Suffocating.

"Mama, I think I know what this is about. It isn't you," Milos said. He was trying to deflect, but I was not having it.

"No Milos, it is her! Nothing I do is right!" The flood gates were fully open, as more tears streamed down my bare cheeks.

"You promised you wouldn't tell her, and now you have brought us to this." Milos looked at me as if I had betrayed him.

It took me a moment to process what he was talking about. Aha. He thought my frustration was with his voyeuristic tendencies. I had promised not to tell her, as it was embarrassing enough for him. He was the one bringing it up.

"Fine, tell her, Brittani, I can't believe you," he practically spit at me.

Again, I wasn't planning on saying anything, but the cat was out of the bag.

"Did you know that your son was watching porn? During my entire pregnancy? I was a virgin when I met him, I haven't been with anyone else, and he was watching porn."

As my chest started to rack with sobs, I took Misha out of the carrier and laid him on the bed next to my mom. Not wanting, even then, to wake him.

"Milos!" exclaimed Zora, disappointed in her son, but not surprised.

Turning to me, she plainly stated, "Brittani, he is a man."

"Your son was on live webcams doing God knows what! And that is okay?"

Him being a man was not a satisfactory answer.

"What do you want? Do you want us to leave?" Zora huffs.

Woah, slow down. No one had said anything about leaving.

Looking at Misha on the bed next to my mom, she was now enraged.

"My baby!" she yelled, pointing at Misha.

Oh, hell no.

Standing up, I got right in her face. I was a good two feet taller than Zora. Time to make something very clear, once and for all.

"No, he is my son!"

The hairy mole on the left corner of her mouth twitched.

She stormed out, went into her room, and grabbed her suitcase. Throwing her clothes in, she continued yelling in Serbian, a few cuss words for sure, as Milos had already taught me the basics.

My fiancé's face was blank. Not happy, not sad, not angry, or concerned.

"Do you want us to go?" he inquired.

If I was being honest, the answer was yes.

I nodded my head.

December 11, 2016

Milos moved out of the townhouse with Zora and Lui.

My heart shattered.

Chapter 12

CANCER

I was so confused. I felt like I had failed. I was devastated, but also relieved. Heartbroken, but furious. My birth had been ruined and the first week thus far had been pure torture. None of it was fair.

I had fought so hard to come to terms with my pregnancy.

The house I had loved was sold, all of my friends were in Los Angeles, and I was again running out of money while waiting for Milos to finally be able to chip in. Now, I wasn't even sure if we were still together.

Yup, rock bottom.

December 12, six days after giving birth, I texted Milos first, practically begging for him to come back. Even inviting Zora as well, if it meant he would just come home and talk. Not even knowing they had also taken Lui until the front door had shut.

I reserved my tears for when Misha was asleep, as the pain was almost unbearable.

Made worse by the fact that Milos, a doctor, said I couldn't leave the house with Misha until he was at least one month old for fear of disease invading his delicate immune system. All I had to do all day was wait, stuck in my own living hell.

Exiled mother and son didn't show up until the next day, dropping by for twenty minutes and leaving again. Milos seemed to be enjoying the emotional torture. He wanted to punish me for kicking him out. More so for kicking out his mom, whatever; in his mind, I needed to be put in my place.

Momma's boy to the max.

Fluids were leaking from at least three places on my body, my stiches hurt from the tearing any time I attempted to sit, there was purple bruising under my eyes from sleep deprivation, and my boobs were covered in abrasions from Misha's attempts to nurse before I gave in and started pumping. And why stop there? I kept having hot flashes as my hormones tried to regulate.

Milos didn't care.

Why didn't he?

Why didn't he care about Misha?

Were these games really necessary?

By December 15, I was going insane. Ninety-six hours spent praying, and hoping, worrying, and crying. Breaking.

I pleaded with him on the phone to come over, talk to me, forgive me for anything I had done wrong. The only thing that could stop my hurting was him.

"I don't think I can come," he said. "My mom is making dinner for Mary and Kevin. I have to go buy bread."

Mary and Kevin were Zora's cousins, if you remember, the ones he was renting the house from back when he lived in San Diego when we first met.

Great, and I would be paying for the bread. He was still using the debit card linked to my checking, which was driving me nuts. I started pulling up my bank account online multiple times a day, seeing where he had been and what he had purchased.

Milos's explanation was that his mom was footing the bill for two hotel rooms at the Rancho Milago Inn. A fancy, boutique hotel with an award-winning restaurant and spa. Milos couldn't very well ask her for money for gas and toothpaste when she was spending close to four thousand dollars a week.

And the car he was driving was still the one that I was paying the lease on.

I was emotionally suffering, financially supporting him when we no longer lived together, and he was concerned with groceries?

Yup, rock bottom.

I told him I didn't want to live. I told him that I was in so much pain, and I needed him to just come home. I needed him to talk to me and fix things. The anguish I was feeling was beyond anything I had ever experienced. I needed him, and he needed to buy bread.

"Milos, we are done. Return the keys, the car, my debit card. I mean it, we're through," I said with finality.

By this time, it was close to midnight. Misha was asleep in his crib, and my mom was awake, the dark marks under her eyes becoming a twin to my own.

"Are you okay?" she asked, concern in her eyes. She must have overheard our conversation.

No, but I stayed silent.

"You should never have to beg someone to love you," she said.

With that sentence, my mother was trying to get through to me. I knew she was right, but I just wanted to take a shower and be alone.

Turning on the water, I rotated the handle to a comfortable temperature. Standing under the steady stream, I let it wash over me as I cried. It wasn't a game, what I had just said on the phone to Milos. I had meant it. Enough with limbo, I had to put our relationship somewhere and that somewhere was splitsville.

Click, the door opened, startling me. Milos walked in and closed it, a smile on his face.

It wasn't a nice smile. Nothing about this smile was warm and friendly. He was enjoying my agony.

"Why were you screaming like that?" he asked, referring to my last words before I had hung up, roughly twenty minutes earlier.

How dare he let himself in uninvited. I refused to be ashamed by my bruised and battered nakedness. Facing him like I was fully decked in armor, not just my skin, I didn't cower.

"Because we are done! Give me my fucking debit card and keys!"

He laughed. "Brittani, I came to you and the kid."

If he wanted to watch, fine, I grabbed the shampoo and started to wash my hair.

"No, this is all your rules, and control. I am done!"

"Brittani, I am studying."

Not able to contain my fury, my body shook with rage.

"Your studying is more important than a child? Because you were watching porn, for months! You're a fucking idiot!"

He was still smiling. I just wanted to smack his face. Words hurt, but people's actions sometimes sting harder. Nothing was making sense anymore. We were engaged, had a baby, and now he was standing in a bathroom, enjoying me crumble.

"I told you I want to die! I told you I want to die, and you are going to buy bread? Fuck you. Leave. Get out. Give me the car, take a fucking taxi home!"

Still calm, in control, he thought all of this was a joke.

"Didn't we have a deal? I would get to finish my boards?"

It was always about him.

"Milos, I just had a baby, fuck your boards."

Sorry for all the expletives—I am not big on cussing—but some situations warrant the use of such language. No need to type out the whole conversation, but there was more yelling, more Milos laughing and brushing it off.

Now I was out of the shower and wrapped in a towel. He approached me and gave me a hug. Treating me like a spoiled child that had just thrown a tantrum, condescending. Hating myself for it, I wanted him to hug me. His fingers ran through my wet hair, massaging my scalp as I cried.

"Shhhh, this is only temporary. I love you. Give me time to study, and I will be back by Christmas." His dry lips touched my wet mouth, sweet, assuring.

I didn't want to give into him, but my mind was saying one thing and my heart another.

I loved him, even then.

Knowing that there was an end date to this nightmare gave me renewed hope. I had taken a break from YouTube, but it was time to jump back in. Not only for monetary reasons, but because I just plain missed making videos and the online interactions.

With Milos and Lui gone, it was tricky. I had to vlog when Milos decided to drop by, pretending we were still living together under one roof. This was his idea. I also had to explain Lui's absence, making some lame excuse like, "Lui was at a friend's house to play with their dogs and that was why he wasn't in the videos." Stating on camera that I had been overwhelmed with the baby and our puppy was being neglected, all of which was a lie.

I think I missed Lui even more than I missed Milos. That lump of fur and I had bonded. We just clicked, and he had been a steady and smelly companion.

My baby daddy, when he did come over, only wanted to see me. He blamed my mother for everything, looking for a scapegoat in all of this instead of our combined mistakes. I kept hoping that he would take an interest in his son, because I wanted Misha to feel wanted. By both of his parents.

Could it be that Milos was jealous of the baby? All of my attention was on the little guy now, which couldn't be helped. I have since heard from multiple women that their partner or husband was competitive with their offspring when they first came home. It kind of makes sense, women carry the children, men help create them. A mother has been a mother for the entire period of development, while a father becomes a father when the child is born.

Maybe he just needed time to fall in love with Misha.

Milos just kept wanting to go out to dinner, or grab coffee, just the two of us. It was getting annoying, as this also meant him leaving Zora with my mom, and my mom having to protect Misha from Zora—alone.

The adoration that I harbored for my European man was dissipating, and I think Milos felt it, too. Our relationship couldn't survive this; too much had happened to be able to recover. You don't just marry an individual, you marry the family, and the thought of a lifetime around Zora just killed it.

His control over me was lessening, no matter what tactics he tried.

Then, one night out of nowhere, Milos started making threatening statements as we sat in his parked car.

"Let's go to court, see what the court says. I will get custody of Misha," he proclaimed.

Milos kept wanting to separate me. From our son, from my mom. He wanted to get me alone so he could berate me without prying eyes or ears. He was trying to figure out which twisted buttons to push to win back some sort of hold.

Panic. They had money to burn, I didn't.

"Fine, if you want to go that route, let's do it," I stated, calling his bluff. Not that it didn't petrify me to my core.

We weren't married, he wasn't a US citizen, and his family was involved in organized crime. I wasn't a legal expert, but I was pretty sure—even with a bad lawyer—that I would have a strong case.

What terrified me wasn't what would happen in court, but what could potentially happen out of it. Would his family retaliate if I stood my ground?

Milos, of course, backed down. Empty threats. I knew that he was still in love with me, but he had Zora whispering in his ear. Putting thoughts into his head and stirring up trouble instead of trying to heal.

Christmas came and went, and Milos was still living at the hotel with Zora.

"I need to study, Brittani. When I finish my boards," he promised anew.

The day after Christmas, Milos was back at the townhouse, and guess what? Yelling, again. Forcing my mom to take Misha in the other room and let me handle it, he verbally pummeled me for hours. Zora was having heart issues because she wasn't getting to spend enough time with her grandson. I didn't understand—they had received multiple invitations to move back in and fix things, but to no avail.

Like a twisted version of *Groundhog Day*, my daily life was on repeat: wake up, love my child, get screamed at, cry myself to sleep.

In all his rages, there was eventual calm. He had worked out whatever the heck he was feeling and wanted to make amends. He said he loved me. That I was his soulmate. "Everything is going to be okay." Blaming his outbursts on something external, like his stress level with his second board exam only four days away.

After most verbal altercations came intimacy. He wanted physical contact, to make out, to try to get me to mess around. I fell for it the first few times, wanting so desperately for any form of comfort and kindness from him.

Over a week of this behavior—fight, hook up, fight, hook up—was starting to make me feel dirty and used.

Giving into what he wanted, just so he would stop yelling.

One of these nights, Nikola and his stolen money popped into my head.

"Whatever happened to Arthur?" I inquired.

Milos froze, but didn't shy away from my question.

"Arthur is no more."

Thump, thump, my heart.

"What do you mean 'no more.' Is he dead?"

Shrugging, as if this was normal, he stated, "Of course, Brittani. Nikola and his business partners couldn't let him get away with what he had done. There were consequences."

Thump, thump, thump. I was silent, but he continued talking.

"I have killed people. I have seen bodies nailed to the wall. Heads in soup," he reflected.

Milos said all of this casually, as if he was talking about the weather, not murder. Suddenly, I wanted to vomit. He had promised me before that he had never killed anyone or committed any crimes that put someone in harm's way. Did he just lie to get me to fall for him?

"Nikola had a promotion, he is now the head of the Serbian Mafia," he concluded.

I had to be smart. I had to play this right.

"Nice," was all I could muster.

During our eye-opening—to say the least—conversation, he told me to watch *The Whistleblower* if I wanted to know what his family was really like. It was a movie from 2011 with Rachel Weisz about a UN peacekeeper who exposed human trafficking that occurred after the Bosnian War.

What the fuck had I gotten myself into?

You probably have been wondering how I have been so detailed, knowing the dates of when events transpired. Around this time, I started taking notes, writing down every instance of yelling, screaming, and violent behavior.

Just in case I would ever need it.

December 27, 2016

Milos was back, ranting, and out of control. He was a handsome man visually, but his behavior was making him hideous. Looking at my notes right now, here are some of the highlights of that rendezvous:

"I am starting to resent our son!"

"You want me to fail my board exams."

"You want me to be your bitch forever."

You, the reader, must be thinking, "Yeah, and what did she say to make him so mad? Come on, it takes two to tango." Also, in my notes, is what I had asserted that sparked this particular verbal fire: "I wish things could go back to the way they were."

That. Was. It. And he was off and running.

You see, I could have said the sky was blue and he would have figured out a way to turn it into an attack.

All of his remaining clothes, he grabbed and threw on the ground. Terrified, I curled up in a ball on the bed as he raged. My mom knocked on the door and opened it. She was holding Misha, and at a loss as to how to proceed.

"Misha just pooped, I, I need a diaper and baby wipes," she stuttered.

Milos charged at her, screaming at the top of his lungs, "You get out! You get out! You get out!"

He raised his arm like he was going to strike, but just slammed the door in her face.

By this point, Milos had been extremely verbally abusive, but not physical. Besides the instance when I was still pregnant. Yes, he would get in my face, throw things, or block my way if I tried to leave a room and he wasn't finished berating me.

Things were escalating. He almost hit my mom while she was holding our infant. A truth that I am still ashamed of.

Luckily, there was a period of respite. Milos came down with a severe case of strep throat. Probably all the late nights studying and emotional onslaughts had weakened his health, but I didn't feel sorry for him. Laryngitis was a beautiful side effect. He couldn't yell, and he was too tired from trying to fight off the strep that he had no choice but to back off.

Because he was so sick, he couldn't be around Misha, as it would have been extremely dangerous if our young one contracted whatever germs he was hosting.

Milos was so ill that he ended up having to go to the hospital with Zora. Besides his throat being on fire, the last few times I had seen him, he was having strong pains in his side that wouldn't subside. Tests were run to try and pinpoint the cause of this, as well.

December 30, 2016

The day of his board exams. He came over in the morning, hands shaking, extremely nervous. Guarded, I couldn't help but feel sorry for him, as he repeatedly checked the schedule and fixed his hair. If I didn't have a child with him, I would have been long gone, changed my identity, and lived in a shack somewhere remote.

Whether I liked it or not, for the moment I was stuck with him.

Milos left to take his exam. Milos called me on his breaks, and again after he had finished. Milos was crying.

"Brittani, I have failed. I failed my test. What am I going to do? Zora had to spend thirty thousand dollars for me to be able to do this, and I failed."

All these months of him studying, where I had bought him every book he needed and quizzed him for hours with medical flashcards, and put my needs aside so that he could take practice quiz after practice quiz, and he had failed? I refused to believe it.

"I am sure that you did good, you are just being too hard on yourself," I said. "Now, we wait."

Leaving him wasn't the question...it was how I was going to go about it that was the riddle.

January 6, 2017

I was finally able to get out of the house with my bundle of joy and my very worried mother. We tried to find moments of happiness, like taking Misha to the grocery store for the first time, where he started screeching in the produce section. The broccoli was particularly interesting.

It probably reminded him of my hair in its natural state, but green.

I was testing out what life would be like without Milos, and starting to ask questions such as, "What now?" and "How would it work if I move back to LA alone and with an infant?" Good questions. Healthy questions.

While I was improving, Milos's health was declining. He started limiting his visits, but called and texted often. Describing to me how he kept sweating all night long, changing his shirt over and over again. The strep refused to go away; none of the prescribed antibiotics were making a dent. When I did see him, his weight had dropped at an alarming rate.

On the tightest belt loop, the smallest pants he owned were quickly becoming too big.

January 20, 2017

Milos received his test results back from the hospital screenings performed in late December.

I was playing with Misha, reading him a Dr. Seuss book— his favorite, because he liked how words sounded when they had a melodic or rhythmic pattern. His miniature feet kicking and steady cooing, proclaiming his enjoyment.

My phone was next to me on the bed and started to ring. Milos.

Debating whether or not to answer, I remembered that he had been kinder the past week. Still, I should have sent him straight to voicemail, with what he had put me through, but he also had me worried.

"Hey Milos, what's up?"

At first, I thought he had pocket dialed me, because the other end was quiet.

"Hello? Milos?"

Finally, he responded.

"I have myelofibrosis. Cancer."

Chapter 13

WAKE UP

"When did you find out? Do they know what stage?"

Instant water works. Silent tears streamed down my face.

His voice was dejected, hopeless.

"I had suspected when I wasn't getting better before my boards. You know how my spleen was swollen? Before Christmas?"

A lot of his conduct was starting to make sense. Milos had been totally unhinged for weeks. Driving like a maniac, picking fights left and right, attacking and attacking, wanting a partner in his sorrow.

Please God, not again. I had watched cancer take my father, and it was ugly and merciless.

"Can you come over? Or are you busy?" I asked.

Everything was forgiven. Wiped clean in an instant, because now I understood. The poor guy had been carrying this burden alone, terrified and in denial. I could only imagine the thoughts that must have been running through his head.

Milos agreed to drop by and he hung up.

Not wanting to move, I felt so powerless.

"Mom, can you come in here?" I managed to say.

I conveyed to her the sad news, and great, now all of us were crying. Except for Misha, who was gurgling and looking around. Too little to understand the hard parts that make up life.

After grabbing my laptop and reading a few articles about myelofibrosis, it was even more soul-crushing. In most instances, it occurs when you are fifty-five and older. Milos's case was rare, as he was only in his twenties. An aggressive form of cancer, treatment options were limited.

The median survival rate, depending on a few factors, was two to eight years.

A sick family member either unifies or divides, and in our case, it brought us all together. Bittersweet, it felt like a cruel joke. Things just kept getting worse when I thought they couldn't possibly.

Milos did drop by that day, while my mom watched Misha in her room. Clinging to each other, I felt Milos's heart pounding as tears from his eyes dampened my cheeks. Studying his beautiful face, my soul was in agony. Milos was so young, so smart, and with so much promise. Why would God, or the universe, do this to me? To him? What had we possibly done so wrong to deserve the misfortune that seemed to plague us at every turn?

If you are going to be sick, you might as well be sick with money.

Zora to the rescue.

She told me she would start transferring cash right away, as all of Milos's treatments were going to be out of pocket. The best option was immunotherapy, and it wasn't covered by insurance. They were looking at five to eight thousand a week, easily.

There wasn't much his oncologists could do, but they had seen some success with prolonging life. The key being to find the right combination of drugs to fight his specific mutations.

Milos started sleeping each night back at the townhouse. More and more of this clothing reunited with the waiting shelves. Where Milos went, Lui was close behind, and I finally had all my boys back under the same roof.

He promised he would fully move back in once my mom was gone, because it wouldn't be fair to Zora if he was living with us again and she was at a hotel.

Honorable. I understood.

Right on cue, Barbara bought her plane ticket home. Wanting to give us the space we were going to need to try and heal, in more ways than one. The father of my child was extremely ill and it was time to really be a family, just the three of us. And Lui.

The closer it came to my mom's migration, the sadder I became. She had been my rock for over four months. It was obvious how much she loved Misha, and it was killing her that she would have to make her exit, which was killing me to watch it kill her.

"Do you want me to stay at a hotel? For a few weeks? Make sure everything is fine before I go?" she asked, loading items into the sterilizer while I watched Misha in his crib on the baby monitor, enthralled with colored objects spinning above him.

"No way, you have already lost months of income because of me. I will not have you spending any more money."

As much as I wanted her to stay, I had to figure out my extremely complicated relationship on my own.

January 29, 2017

Misha was having serious reflux, which was fairly normal in bottle-fed babies. He had to sleep at an incline, or the contents of his stomach would keep coming up and he would fuss and fuss. My wonderful mother had stayed awake all night, holding him on her chest in-between feedings so he could have some relief from his developing digestive system.

I wanted to drive her to the airport, but she insisted on catching a cab. We just had to pull off the Band-Aid.

Hug, a kiss for Misha, more tears, and she was off.

I had never felt so alone.

Milos was over within an hour, upbeat and optimistic. His cheekbones were more pronounced. The angles of his face, striking, with his continued weight loss. Carrying a duffle bag full of his remaining belongings, he dropped it on the floor next to our bed.

Lui bounded in the doorway after him, transporting one of a dozen tennis balls scattered throughout our nest. Begging Milos to play fetch.

Our puppy associated the master bedroom with fun. I would sit on the bed with Misha, so he was safe, and throw the tennis ball over and over down the hallway for Lui to retrieve. That dog didn't care where he got to play or if the scenery didn't change, as long as there was someone to play with.

"Did Barbara leave already?" Milos asked, already knowing the answer.

"Yes, about an hour ago."

His faces wrinkled in concern. "Why didn't you tell me? I would have given her a ride!"

He had enough on his plate, not that I wanted to treat him any differently.

"It is all good. Are you hungry?"

Milos was famished, another side effect of the cancer. No matter how much he consumed, he was still losing weight.

We hit up a popular restaurant in Carmel Valley with our son. Our first family outing. No matter how hard I tried that afternoon, I couldn't hide the sadness I felt now that the one person who always had my back was gone. Milos tried to make small talk in between bites, digging into his steak.

My mind kept zoning out, weary and burdened.

There had been so much energy expended. I could have slept for a week and still been drained.

Milos was getting more and more irritated with my silence.

After lunch, we had made plans to pick up groceries, and then head home. Wanting to sit next to Misha, so he wasn't alone in the backseat, my maybe fiancé was driving. Spotting me in the rear-view mirror, his tempter started to flare.

"What is wrong with you?" he demanded. "You want your mommy, not me. You just want me to die."

Hurtful, hurtful words. Gosh, I was sick of crying, the wet stains marring the makeup that I wore so rarely these days.

"That is not true, stop it," I said.

He pulled a sudden U-turn in the middle of an intersection. Holding onto Misha's car seat, my knuckles were white. My SUV zoomed back towards the townhouse, away from the market.

"Brittani! I have fucking cancer! I am dying! And you don't care!"

Every word was a dagger, sharply stabbing into me. Nothing could have been farther from the truth!

"Milos, please don't yell! Misha!"

Our precious son was starting to fuss and squirm, not understanding the raised voices.

Where we were located in Carmel Valley, everything was a short drive, so it wasn't long before we were parked in front of the townhouse. He flipped off the engine and turned to face me.

Furious.

"Do you know one of the causes of cancer? Stress!"

He slammed his hand on the center console, causing me to jump.

"You and your mom gave me fucking cancer! I am dying, and you don't give a shit."

If you have ever been in a seriously traumatic situation, everything seems to slow down. What is another word for devastated? Ruined? Annihilated? Smashed? Crushed? Everything that we had gone through so far was nothing compared to this.

I needed to get Misha out of that car before Milos started driving again. He was out of control. Unlocking Misha's car seat, I quickly exited the car, and carried him inside. Wanting to get somewhere that I could protect him.

A monster, not a man, followed us up the stairs, spewing hate with every step. Had he not destroyed me enough? Had I not paid enough?

Like a switch being flipped, now Milos was crying.

"You just want me to die so you can marry someone else."

Misha was laying in his crib. His fussing had stopped as he focused intensely on his mobile. Trying harder and harder to grab the odd spinning contraptions.

Before I could stop him, Milos scooped our son into his arms. Holding him, kissing his head. His mood changed again, the anger returning as he held our son.

"What? Is it wrong that I hold him? I have every right to hold him!"

Fear clenched my chest, but I had to try to keep him docile while he was grasping our infant.

"You fucked this up. You have fucking postpartum depression! You and your fucking hormones caused all of this!"

Now he was pacing, spewing whatever combination of words he thought would sting the most.

"I just want to spend what little time I have left with my son! You know what is fucked up? When I do die, you won't let any of my family see him! I am the one that convinced you not to have an abortion!"

Spit was flying. He was grinding his teeth with unbridled fury. His eyes were wide and manic.

Misha was crying.

I had to stop him.

Making a split-second decision, I ran to the office, pulled my phone out of my purse, and threw my messenger bag onto the bed. As I started to dial 911, Milos was behind me, grabbing my wrist and wrenching the phone from my hand. Blinding pain shot up my wrist and arm, my left pinky receiving the worst of it.

I screamed and screamed for help. Our neighbors in the attached unit were only a thin wall between us, but they must not have been home.

Déjà vu.

Only this time, it was just me being hurt.

Sliding down to the floor, Milos put my phone into his pocket and extracted his own. My baby was wailing and I was completely helpless. The monster was stronger, having a good hundred pounds of muscle on me. With only one free hand and arm, he had overpowered any resistance with ease.

"Look at you, I am recording you. You need to get treatment."

Smiling again, a smile full of malice. When it came to fights, Milos kept going and going until he thought he had won. I had to make him think that he had won. I had to get him to calm down and give me Misha.

"You're right. I think I do have postpartum. This has all been my fault. I am so sorry."

Crying harder and harder and he was laughing. Standing over me as I huddled on the carpet floor, defeated.

It took a few hours, but Milos relaxed and gave Misha back to me, apologizing. He didn't want to die, and all of this had just been really hard on him. With Milos, it was always the stick and then the carrot. Sheepishly, he also returned my phone. My left hand was throbbing; the knuckle on my pinky was swollen and had easily doubled in size.

I didn't think anything was broken, besides me.

Needing to change my sweatpants because Misha had spit up, I had Milos hold the baby as I went into the walk-in closet to swap for a fresh pair. Quickly pulling out my phone, I snapped two photos of my injury and changed my lock screen password, just in case.

My mom made it back to Arizona safely, and I didn't want to be any more of a burden. I just told her that we had gotten into a little fight, but everything was going to be okay.

"Milos is just scared out of his mind and really needs you right now," she explained.

Sneakily, I had been messaging her when Milos left the room. She was right, but it didn't make my life any easier.

I no longer felt alone, I was alone.

Sleep evaded me. Milos moaned and drenched shirt after shirt with sweat, well into the following morning. His body was trying to fight off the cancer by burning it up. Raising his

temperature to a high enough level, his immune system struggled to kill the quickly multiplying invaders.

The more time I had to think, the more I realized his outburst
was my fault as well.

If I only had been more tolerant of Zora, and never kicked
them out, this wouldn't have happened.

The blame was on me.

My self-esteem was at an all-time low and I was willing to do
anything to make it right.

Anything to stop the fighting.

Even if it meant letting Zora back in.

We started slowly, with her staying for an afternoon and
Milos returning her back to the hotel at night. She really was a
talented cook, obvious by her girth, and I was too busy with our
one-month-old to be able to fix the kind of meals Milos needed.

No sugar, low salt, veggies, and, with his type of cancer,
meat.

Anemia was an unwelcome friend, so Milos had to incorpo-
rate liver into his diet for the iron.

We received a bit of good news before he started his immunotherapy treatments: further blood draws and analysis and the
doctors now thought he had chronic lymphoblastic leukemia,
not myelofibrosis like they first suspected.

"I am going to be all good in two, three months, and then we
can put this behind us. We will be in Serbia, getting married."

He kissed the hand he was holding.

I no longer wanted to marry him, but how do you abandon
someone fighting for their very existence? What if it were me
that had cancer and not him? There was only one option. Stay.

Having to be up and pumping milk multiple times a night,
I frequently got lost browsing medical articles. Learning about

the drugs he was on, various treatments, and their success rates. Some of the best cancer hospitals were in Texas, or back east, and I didn't understand why he was messing around.

He had the resources to be able to get premium, cutting-edge treatment. Why not go where they had the highest cure rates?

"Brittani, Zora keeps having to pay so much in fees to transfer cash for my treatments. Do you think we could send money to your checking account?"

If it would help, why not? But I had to ask my accountant first. It was now late February, and things had been relatively smooth between Milos and I for almost a month.

Enduring his treatments alone, because Misha was too small to be at the hospital and around the potential germs, he had me constantly worried. Sometimes they had to keep him hospitalized for two, three days at a time, when his body wasn't handling the drugs. He did better when they administered Interferon Alpha only, as it made his muscles ache as well as some vomiting. Nothing compared to when it was a Rituxan day.

Rituxan, or Rituximab, was intense, attacking the unhealthy cells and mercilessly destroying them. The result was that his whole body felt like it was on fire. Milos's heart, pounding. Pounding so loud I thought it might burst as my head rested on his chest, trying to offer what comfort I could muster.

He kept talking about death. Everything I had been reading said your attitude was just as important as the treatment itself. Milos was giving up too easily.

"Can you do something for me? I already have your passport, but I need Misha's social security card and birth certificate. You know my apartment in Russia? And the office building I own in Serbia? My lawyer is going to draw up paperwork. Both go to

Misha when he is eighteen. Well, if I die, they would go to both of you right away."

His miserable outlook only added to my misery.

"You aren't going to die! Come on! This isn't necessary," I replied, a sunny grin on my face. The mask I now wore. Upbeat, over-positive, pretend housewife.

Milos inquired day after day about Misha's documents, insisting that he wanted us taken care of "just in case."

On February 22, I relented. Giving him all the paper items necessary to set his affairs in order.

His doctors now believed that his cancer was no longer chronic, but acute lymphoblastic leukemia. Wasting away, in more and more pain, it was apparent that his body wasn't responding to treatments as they had hoped. Could the universe not throw us a bone? Maybe Milos was being punished for his past indiscretions, bad karma, but I hated having to witness it.

More and more crying. He finally did get his step one board results back, and he did indeed fail. But only by a few points. Showing me the email proof on his laptop, he had scored lowest in pathology. Odd, as his master's degree was in forensic pathology.

"My first language is Serbian, my medical schooling was in Serbian and German, and I have to translate the questions from English. How is this possible? How could I have missed so many?" he demanded. He looked to me for answers. His beautiful, sad eyes looked to me and I had no clue what to say.

One by one, our plans and dreams had perished.

The extra money from the sale of my house was going to last, potentially, three more months if I was careful.

Milos was defeated, and now, so was I.

I couldn't take any more bad news.

Through of all of this I continued to make the YouTube vlogs that had brought so much success to my channel. Continued to film and upload my adorable little family, knowing that sooner or later the comments would start changing.

"Why is Milos so thin?"

"Is Milos okay?"

"Your fiancé is getting skinny! Girl, get him to eat more!"

"Is Milos alright? He looks sick."

Here's a morbid thought. If Milos did lose this battle with cancer, his son would have videos to watch of his father. Knowing him through a computer screen would be better than not knowing him at all.

I was emotionally, physically, and monetarily taking care of everyone. No one was taking care of me.

Every time I was on the phone with my mother, or even mentioned her name, he tensed up. Still angry, he blamed her for stolen time and adding to the stress that made his body sick.

I could only talk to her was when he was at his treatments. It felt like I had to sneakily communicate, which was driving me mad. Not fair, as I had been working on forgiving Zora. It was still a power struggle, she was still a controlling pig, but I had been polite and kind and made an effort to find common ground.

Unable to stand it any longer, sick or not, I decided to bring it up one evening.

Milos was having a pleasant day, not overly nauseated or weak. It seemed like the right timing.

"As you know, I have been making an effort with Zora. I would like you to do the same with my mother," I said, rubbing his head. Misha was already zonked, snoring gently in his crib.

"Absolutely not," he answered without hesitation.

My hands stopped, not expecting the topic to still be so touchy.

"Milos, I can only talk to her when you are not around or I get glares and weird looks. She is my mother! The one that paid off your first car so I could get you the lease for the second. She loves you!"

He was out of bed now, pacing. Things were escalating quickly.

"Stay calm, come on! I am doing everything I can to help! I just want to be able to talk to my mom when you are around!" I said, pleading for him to at least give me this.

"I am sick, Brittani! I am fucking sick! What is wrong with you?"

He went to say more but stopped. Suddenly, Milos grabbed his chest, his eyes wide.

"My heart! My heart! I think I am having a heart attack!"

With that, he fell to the floor. Motionless.

I wanted to laugh. That was the worst acting I had ever seen. Sure, he wasn't moving, but I also wasn't buying it.

Getting up calmly, and stepping over him, I headed towards the kitchen.

"If you had a heart attack, I am going to call for assistance."

No sooner were the words out of my mouth before he was magically stumbling behind me, still holding his chest.

"Get me an ice pack! For my wrists! My heart, Brittani!"

This got my attention.

He was yelling and shaking, stumbling. Maybe he really *was* having a heart attack.

I rushed to the freezer, handed him a blue frozen rectangle, and grabbed my phone. As I dialed 911, he wheezed and pocketed his wallet and keys.

"Milos, wait! We need to call an ambulance!"

Putting the ice pack on his right wrist, he turned and stumbled back down the hallway to the staircase, hitting the walls as he tried to move quickly. Not listening, he kept tripping and falling down the steps.

Now, I was screaming.

"Stop! Wait for an ambulance! What are you doing?"

Milos opened the door at the base of the stairs and practically fell into the night air.

"I am going to drive myself! It will be faster. Take care of Misha."

Struggling to get into his car, I watched him back out swiftly, throwing the sports car into drive and burning rubber.

My teeth were chattering. My body started to shake as I proceeded to call 911 and describe in detail what he was wearing. The make, model, and license plate number of his car. Where he was headed, and what freeway I thought he was on. The nice female dispatcher on the other end assured me that they would do their best to look for him.

What if he had another heart attack on the way to the emergency room and crashed?

But why did I still not believe him?

They released him from the hospital the next day, but according to Milos, he did indeed have a minor heart attack. The doctors urged him to keep his stress levels down, especially with the drugs traveling through his system.

Again, this was my fault.

Enough was enough. I shut down, sinking into depression. Misha was loved, and well cared for, but I stopped caring about my well-being. Showering only every three or four days, brushing my teeth when I remembered. Eating only when my hunger would no longer tolerate my indifference.

I was a shell of the person I once was.

Hollow. Docile. Jumping to please.

Even in the fog I now resided in, things just weren't adding up.

"The doctors want me to go play tennis, workout. It is crucial for blood cancers."

Misha in the stroller, we sat, watching him play. He would run all over the court for two, three hours at a time.

When my dad had cancer, he spent a lot of time resting. Too wiped out most days to do much of anything.

An itch in the back of head just wouldn't go away. It kept itching and itching, urging me to wake up.

March 12, 2017

It was 2:00 a.m. and I was still awake. Misha was like clockwork, wanting to eat at midnight, two o'clock, and then six in the morning.

Milos was having all these treatments, right? But how? What method were they using to deliver the meds?

Good old Google.

I typed in "How is Rituxan administered?"

Opening the official website for the drug, guess what? Injected by IV.

I had an IV in my hand when I was giving birth. It left a nasty bruise for a week.

There wasn't a mark on Milos's flawless, tan, skin.

That motherfucker.

Chapter 14

JUST DO IT

Click, click, click, so many things were falling into place and starting to make sense.

Milos wouldn't let me come with him to any of his doctor's appointments, because he wasn't sick.

He could play tennis and work out for hours at a time, because he wasn't sick.

He didn't want anyone around us to know he had cancer, because they might catch onto him.

He was convinced that he would be cured in two, three months tops because *he* got to decide when this charade ended.

Milos may not have been physically sick, but he was definitely sick in the head. What kind of human fakes having a serious, life-threatening illness and enjoys watching the suffering it causes? Correction, what kind of humans? Zora was in on his lie, playing her part of "concerned parent" flawlessly.

Some examples:

"I have to wait at his appointments, I am so worried."

"He is so young, this is not fair."

"Brittani, don't be sad, he is very tough. He will beat this."

My first guess was that his "cancer" was an elaborate plan to get my mom out of the way and get Zora back in. Some twisted game they were playing to punish me until they thought I had been punished enough.

He could have continued to use "stress" as a reason once he was "cured" to keep us separated, so he wouldn't have a potential relapse.

I had also seen Milos's true colors, and he was dangerous. The verbal abuse and physical altercations had been steadily escalating. Milos was an artist at torturing me, and like any artist, he would want to keep improving in his craft.

"Mom, I think Milos has been faking having cancer," I confessed on the phone.

No gasp, or shock in her voice when she replied, "I could have told you that one."

She further explained that I was so brainwashed and controlled, that she didn't know if I would ever snap out of it. That even if she had told me he was faking his disease, I wouldn't have believed her. Sadly, she was right. I wouldn't have wanted to believe that someone could be that evil. I would have pulled away even further, limiting our contact, choosing to support Milos.

"When did you figure it out?" I asked, trying to deduce the timeline of events.

"I had my suspicions, but I knew for sure when he started playing tennis every few days. You just can't do that, especially if he is going through immunotherapy. He is strong, but not that strong. I haven't been sleeping, I have been so worried about you."

"What do I do now? Tell me what to do, and I will do it."

My mom wanted to immediately jump in her car, drive to the airport, hop on the next plane, and come to our rescue.

But now was not the time to be rash.

We hatched a plan. Barbara would come out for one of her normal antique buying trips, which she had been doing every two to three months since Milos and I had started dating. She had been gone for a month and a half, so the timing was perfect.

I would schedule a few meetings. Appointments to fix the funky haircut and dye job I had received in San Diego. A meeting with a new management company that wanted to represent me and some of my writing projects. Legitimate business-related events in LA that Milos would have no choice but to let me go to, putting a cozy hundred something miles between us.

After all, I was paying all the bills. Milos was bonkers, but not blind. He knew he needed his cash cow to keep earning, so he could keep spending.

We booked the hotels that we were going to be staying at with my mom's credit card, just in case.

"Absolutely not! That woman is not coming back in this house. I don't feel comfortable with her around my son!" Milos shouted.

But, knowing now what he was hiding, I also knew what buttons to push.

"Fine, then we are going to go our separate ways. I need to do this, for work, to earn money. You either get on board, or we break up."

If we were just friends, I would no longer be paying for everything, and he would have to pass his boards and get a job. Granted, it would be a really well-paying job when he did finally succeed, but that would also involve working.

Cancer was the perfect excuse for him to sleep all night long, while I was up with the baby. It was the perfect excuse for him not to have to study anymore and play video games or watch movies. It was the perfect excuse to be on constant holiday, where he could work out, come and go as he pleased, and absolutely everything was taken care of.

We reached a sort of compromise.

Milos decided that we were going to baptize Misha in LA, so he and Zora would come up and meet us after a couple of days. In Serbian Orthodox baptisms, they wrap the baby in oil cloth, full submerge them in water three times, and the godfather cuts his hair.

Milos had also decided that Jurica would be Misha's godfather. The thug lawyer who cheated on his alcoholic, anorexic wife. This I knew to be true, as I had seen Mara drunk on more than one occasion, and overhead conversations between Zora and her about Jurica's infidelity.

Jurica would be an amazing role model for our offspring. Not.

I said yes to his every request, so he would say yes to me leaving town, unsupervised, with our son. It worked. My favorite person on the planet was existing solely on breastmilk, so it was pretty much a given that Misha would be tagging along.

We would get to LA and then figure out what to do next.

Even harder than Milos pretending to be sick, was me pretending that I didn't know that he was pretending. I had to sleep in the same bed, kiss him, rub his back, act normal. Not let him catch on.

What was Nikola going to do when he found out I had left Milos?

And what was Milos ingesting to manifest his symptoms? The sweating all night? The vomiting? Racing heartbeat, swollen glands, a white stripe down the back of his throat, hives, and rashes. He was a doctor, so he probably knew exactly what drugs to take and what dosage.

If I was going to leave Milos, time was of the essence. I needed an excuse as to why I was starting to pack up the townhouse. This part of the plan wasn't too hard to act out, as I really was running out of money, and I really would have had to move. It just gave me the flexibility to be able to start packing up my stuff without raising suspicion.

"We have to get out of this apartment, it is too expensive! I don't care if we have to pay the lease break fee, but I can't afford it any longer!"

A partially genuine statement on my part; I really couldn't afford the money-sucking-dwelling any longer. Milos and I had this conversation as we browsed ingredients at the supermarket for yet another healthy dinner catered to his "affliction," even though I wanted to run, holding Misha and screaming, "Fire, Fire!" at the top of my lungs.

"Whatever you think we need to do, Brittani. We can move to a smaller apartment," he said, buying into my lies for a change.

With that, I started sorting and packing any moment that Misha was sleeping, staying within range of the baby monitor. I might have filled the community dumpster, and I mean the entire dumpster, four times with all my old props and costumes. When you have created over a thousand videos like I had, you unintentionally turn into a hoarder. Halloween was easy, I just had to go into my garage and pick out a costume.

All of it no longer mattered. None of the props, or clothes I owned, or antiques I had collected.

Nice things are nice, but they are just that—things.

I would have thrown everything away if it meant getting out of there sooner.

March 19, 2017

My mom drove from Sedona, Arizona to San Diego. She could have flown, but if we were going to get me moved out of the townhouse, we were going to need the extra mode of transportation.

Milos knew something was up, but he wasn't fully onto me.

As I gave Misha his morning bath, my mom was off loading my car with her suitcases and such. We were going to leave her vehicle, and have it shipped back at a later date.

Milos should have been at one his "treatments," as it was past 9:00 a.m., the time when they were always "scheduled," but his "doctors" were okay with him coming in later that morning after we had headed out.

"You are not going with Misha." Milos was crouched down next to me, as our son tried to splash. From birth, he had loved water, especially if he could stir it up and get it everywhere.

"Leave him with Zora and I," he ordered.

Why was I crying again? I hated and was terrified of this man, but how could I still want him?

For me, this was goodbye.

Lately, whenever he went to his "treatments," he kept coming back tanner and tanner. He said he liked to sit on a bench at the hospital and get fresh air. Uh huh, unless he was sitting on the bench in his underwear, because not just his face was getting darker. He was, of course, lying.

Was he lying every time he told me that he loved me?

Was our whole relationship a lie?

I couldn't worry about that just yet, and my tears were actually a good thing. He was in attack mode so often, weeping was my natural response.

"There is no way that I am leaving Misha and you already agreed to this trip. I mean it, Milos, you be nice to my mom or we will be just friends."

He hesitated, but got up and left, passing Barbara in the hallway.

I heard an overly bright, "Good Morning!" exit his lips. Comical, as he had pretty much ignored her since her arrival.

Finally, my car was packed and we were off.

I wasn't too worried about retaliation the first day, sending photos of Misha and keeping him informed.

My teeth hadn't been looked at in forever, so I desperately needed to hit up my dentist in Beverly Hills. I also wanted to talk to Abbie, the elderly hygienist who had been cleaning my chompers since I was eighteen. She was a grandma herself, many times over, and had given solid advice in the past.

Laying in her chair, I was totally drained as I told her about Milos, the lies, and his mother's actions. Abbie was appalled, but patiently let me recount my woes.

"That woman is going to try to take your son," she said finally. "She really does think that baby is hers! You don't let him out of your sight! And are you sure she is his mom? I mean, they sleep in the same bed. You said she is always rubbing his back or his leg, a bit incestuous don't you think?"

Click, click, click, more things started to fall into place.

Milos and Zora kept insisting that we go to Serbia so everyone could see Misha when he was six months old. At six months, he could be off of breast milk and would no longer need me.

Milos only wanted photos of Misha, never Misha and me.

Zora had already bought a crib and toys for her apartment in Belgrade and their other house in Bosnia.

Milos and I had taken portraits after his "cancer" diagnosis with another cousin of his, Anto. Anto was a professional photographer and lived in Hollywood. He had come down for a weekend, during which Milos also insisted I snap new head-shots for acting as well.

What I had thought odd was that Milos wanted pictures, too. Close up, not smiling, mouth closed, from the shoulders up.

Passport photos.

A myriad of the "headshots" Anto had taken of me were also the same framing.

They could now make fake passports for Milos, Misha, and me.

Milos had tricked me into giving him Misha's social security card and birth certificate, and he already had copies of my passport and driver's license.

Who knows, they could have started applying for Serbian citizenship for Misha, as Serbian law only required the consent of one parent to do so.

Zora and her maybe son had everything they needed to leave the country with my child without my permission.

Whenever Zora was around Misha, she kept mentioning his smooth skin, how he didn't have any birthmarks or any physical imperfections. Shit, were they going to sell my son? They could already have a buyer, and a healthy, attractive male baby would fetch a pretty price tag.

On more than one occasion, Milos had talked about Nikola's friends, who were supposedly involved in human traf-ficking. Another possible reason why Milos had no emotional attachment. His child was just another underhanded business transaction.

I was shivering, but not cold. Abbie hadn't even started cleaning my teeth. I was scared out of my mind, but in protect mode.

"But how do I get out? His family is wealthy and running the Serbian mafia!" I whispered the last part, as anyone else in the dental office would have been like, "What?!?"

My adorable hygienist leaned over me so her face was right in front of mine, pulling her glasses down to convey her next words very clearly.

"You just do it."

Goosebumps lined my arms. She was right.

First things first, I needed to file a police report for the second instance of domestic violence, where he had hyper-extended my pinky finger. The Pasadena police department informed me that it needed to be done in the county of the crime.

Frustrating, as this meant that we had to head back to San Diego prematurely.

My next move on this dangerous chess board was to cancel Misha's christening.

March 22, 2017

"Milos, I have been thinking really hard, and I want to wait on his baptism. What religion and when should be a mutual decision. Something that we decide together," I texted him, fearing his response.

It was immediate.

"You decided with me, I nicely asked and paid and organized. This is a sin, Brittani, and this is your mom again."

Typical Milos manipulation.

"No verbal abuse, it has to stop."

Bubbles on the screen indicated that he was typing. Ding.

"Ok, think about this VERY VERY VERY WELL."

I knew what he was implying. Think about his family, their power and connections. And I did think about it all night long and well into the next morning. Every white van that passed, every stranger who stared or seemed to be watching. At any moment, I fully expected to be kidnapped or worse.

March 23, 2017

The plan continued. This time, ending our relationship for good. I needed Milos fully moved out, the leased car I was paying for returned, as well as all the keys to the townhouse and the debit card he was still using.

While at the hair salon, getting my color fixed, I decide to enact this part of the ruse.

"Our relationship isn't working and hasn't been for a long time. I no longer feel comfortable living with you. I need you to return the Mercedes to the townhouse by tomorrow afternoon and turn in the keys to the front office. They will be expecting you before 4:00 p.m.," I texted him.

Again, his response was immediate.

"Do you want to do it this way then? You want to go this way with me? Think about this as well."

Whatever was to come, I wasn't backing down.

"No more threats."

We went back and forth until he finally relented, knowing that I owned the car and could report it stolen if he didn't comply. He technically was on the lease for the townhouse and didn't have to move out if he didn't want to do so, but thankfully he finally gave in.

March 24, 2017

We packed up the car again and headed back down south. There was no other choice. My only hope was getting the San Diego police involved and going through the legal system, praying that we might find some sort of protection. Something was better than nothing. We weren't married, but Milos was still Misha's father and had legal rights to him until a court clarified custody.

What if we would have just fled the state? Milos and I weren't married, but Misha was still his child by blood. He could have reported his son had been kidnapped, and then I would have been the one in trouble. So, incredibly, discouraging.

What if I would have left Misha in LA with my mother? One, I couldn't afford a hotel week after week, and neither could she. And two, what if the court ordered mandatory visitation? I would not be able to move out of San Diego county without a judge's permission.

Reason three, we were better off together than divided. Even if it meant entering back into the lion's den.

Normally I loved road trips, but the hundred-and-twenty-mile journey back to San Diego was the worst of my existence. Not knowing if Milos had done as I had asked and moved out. Not knowing what was waiting for us.

Pulling up to the townhouse, I saw that Milos had indeed left the car in the driveway. Filthy, dirty, and with a few extra thousand miles. I had no clue where he had been driving to rack it up so quickly. Mexico and back? Best guess.

Even more disturbing, he somehow left the house keys and the debit card on the stairs, but managed to lock the front door, which told me that he had an extra set.

Immediately I called the police, explained my situation, and waited for an officer to arrive.

My mom tried to warn me, as her uncle was chief of police in Montana while she was growing up. She knew first-hand how most law enforcement officers operate.

"Whoever comes is going to be really hard on you, because they are trained to do so in domestic violence cases. They have to make sure that you are telling the truth."

Oh boy, was she right. Officer Miller was a stone-cold individual. In his forties, with blonde hair that was fashioned into a buzz cut. He looked like he was probably ex-military, the hardened persona that follows most soldiers who have experienced live combat.

"Why are you reporting this over a month after it occurred? Why didn't you call us right away? Explain to me exactly why I should believe you."

His voice was flat, emotionless.

"Because it's the truth."

Officer Miller drilled me and drilled me until I started to give up. If I couldn't convince him of the facts, then I was on my own. Milos would get to brainstorm and enact whatever revenge he deemed suitable for my latest disobedience.

When he finished questioning me, I took Misha to my bedroom, so he could now interrogate my mother. Find out her take on things and the events that had occurred. Barbara had also warned me about this as well, that we would be separated and questioned individually to make sure that everything lined up.

My shoulders slumped as I stared out the tiny window next to the bed in the dwelling that had been my own personal purgatory.

Footsteps indicated the officer was walking through the hallway, and back down the steps. My mom opened the bedroom door, peeking her head in. "He said he would be right back."

Barbara, Misha, and I sat on the couch in the living room in silence. Our spirits were low as we waited.

It felt like an hour before Officer Miller did indeed plod back up the stairs, paperwork in hand.

"I am not sure if a domestic violence restraining order will be granted, as you waited so long to report the crime. I have made a report, here is the number, call here to find out when it will be ready for pickup. Take your report number and head to the San Diego courthouse on Monday, get there early, see if they will give you some temporary orders of protection."

I thanked him and thanked him, hoping that it wasn't too late.

His parting words at the door were as follows:

"Change the locks. Tell your neighbors what is going on, in case they spot him in the neighborhood, so they can warn you. Do not go anywhere alone, don't go out after dark unless it is an emergency. Good luck."

Luck—I was gonna need it.

Chapter 15

SOCIOPATH

March 27, 2017

"Mom! My birth certificate! I had two official copies, one is missing!"

My mother had just gotten out of the shower and Misha had been crying and fussy since 5:00 a.m., refusing that any of us sleep a second longer.

She was fully dressed with a towel wrapped around her hair as her face drained of color.

"Great. Just great. Call the police, again."

All of my important documents had been stuffed in the bottom of the blanket box at the base of my bed. Having chosen not to be there when Milos had transported his items, I thought it best to check on things that were valuable and make sure they were still accounted for.

Another officer of the law, this time a very bubbly brunette, wrote down my account of the stolen certificate. Giving me the document number and specifying when it would be available at the San Diego Police department records office, she took her leave.

The moment she exited, my phone rang. It was the detective at the police department assigned to my domestic violence case. He was giving me a follow-up call, to see if I had any further questions.

"What do you think he was on to assist in his cancer act? What kind of drugs?" I inquired, hoping he would lend some clarity.

The gruff male voice pondered a moment. "He probably is using cocaine, or heroin. All he would need to do is go off of the drugs, and his body would head into withdrawals, causing the night sweats and more."

Milos used to always talk about how "every surgeon used cocaine" because they needed it to be able to "work for eighteen hours straight." At least some of his erratic behavior made more sense. He was likely on drugs. Whether they were illegal, prescription, or over the counter, I wasn't sure. I had never seen him taking anything in person, but he was constantly wiping or blowing his nose.

My now ex-fiancé also had high blood pressure, weight loss, vomiting, increased heart rate—a myriad of symptoms that coincided with some sort of substance abuse.

I was the third person in line at the courthouse after an already busy morning. San Diego's judicial system had certain times where you could get help with paperwork from paralegals on the courthouse staff for free. Yes, I needed a lawyer, but I could get the ball rolling on my own.

I didn't think Milos would try anything at such a public venue, surrounded by law enforcement, so I felt somewhat safe for the moment.

When the doors opened at 8:00 a.m., like dominoes, we fell one by one in an orderly fashion through the aged double doors. Before I knew it, I was in front of a very sweet paralegal.

Sporting not a lick of makeup, and her curly auburn hair pulled back in a ponytail, she was a no fuss kind of gal. After I recounted my story yet again, she condensed it to the key elements, typing away as I talked. Mafia, abuse, rage, fear that they might flee the country with my son: all valid reasons why I needed a restraining order. This, in turn, was sent to a judge to see if he or she would grant my request.

From there, I was shuffled to another department to wait for the magistrate's decision.

Three excruciating hours I lingered, in a very uncomfortable chair, in front of the clerks on the third floor.

"Brittani Taylor? Come to window two, please."

I could feel my chest clench as I walked, barely daring to breathe.

The employee at the standing desk was Chinese American, probably about my age, and kind-natured. He had a warm smile and empathic demeanor about him. Everyone I had encountered so far had been friendly, but professional. Whoever did the hiring, bravo.

"Your temporary restraining order has been granted. The orders need to be served by a third party, the Sheriff's office, a friend, or using a substitute service. It needs to be done before your first court date on 4-17-2017."

Relieved, I thanked him and called my mom to give her the good news. Booking it back to my car, I only felt secure once I was inside with the doors locked.

All we needed to do now was figure out how to get him served.

Here was my hunch. Milos had told me he was staying with his mom, in a hotel, at the Rancho Milago Inn, right? But Zora always seemed to be bringing over food that she had made. Soups, bread, baklava. According to Milos, she was cooking everything at his Aunt Mary's house and bringing it over.

Lui was always playing with—correction, humping—his aunt's dogs. Could it be that Milos and Zora were staying with Mary and Kevin?

Kevin Adams, her husband, had added me on Facebook months earlier. Home, and back on the computer, I typed into a search engine: "Kevin Adams address San Diego." One of the first two generic background check websites pulled it up, no problem. There was a photo of Kevin, as well as his phone number, home address, and other personal information for a minimal fee.

Betting on the website information being accurate, I filled out the necessary paperwork and dropped it off at the Sheriff's office for them to pursue.

I was right. Milos was served the next day.

He had guilted me for months and months about how expensive the hotel was because I had kicked out Zora, and the whole time they were staying with his aunt for free. When I had asked why Zora wasn't staying with Mary, Milos said that she couldn't because they had an "exchange student."

Zora was enrolled in an English school and had started taking classes to improve her language skills. My guess was that their exchange student and Zora were one and the same.

Masters of manipulation.

No longer numb and controlled, I was wide-awake and fighting for the freedom and safety of not only myself, but my mother and my child.

If I ever decided to become a detective, I would probably be pretty good at it. Love had made me trusting and naive. Now, I was tireless in my pursuit of the truth and anything that would help me win. The stakes were too high not to.

With the court date fast approaching, I needed to not only move out of the townhouse, with most of my remaining belongings going into storage, but I also desperately needed to find a good family lawyer. Someone who could convince the judge that I should be allowed to leave the state with my child to an address only disclosed to the court. Assuring the powers that be that I wasn't running and would be present at any and all future trial dates.

Having never had to hire a lawyer before, good 'ole Mom stepped in to help and she found one on Yelp.

"Brittani, how about this place? It looks really good!"

She was pointing to a family law practice on the computer screen, Axle Law Group. Reviews on Yelp and sites like it were reliable, as people were brutally honest. If they loved a business, they loved it, and if they hated it, you would know exactly why. Review after review of this particular establishment were glowing.

I dialed right away and a young woman answered. She wasted no time, asking me my court date and routine questions about my case, then proceeding to put me on hold.

After a couple of minutes, I heard her voice again.

"Can you come by in an hour for a consult? I am going to have you meet with Jenny Phillips, she is one of our lawyers. Bring the restraining order, police report, anything that you have for our files."

I did just that. Exactly one hour later, I was sitting in their conference room and anxiously waiting. My foot tapping the floor, I held tight to the stack of evidence I had compiled so far.

In walked Jenny, and I instantly liked her. She was full Irish, a tiny, feisty little thing. Long, curly brown hair, porcelain skin, and a heart-shaped face with dark blue eyes. Within a few minutes of talking, it was obvious that she was competent, professional, and experienced.

"Which judge do you have? Linden? I really like him. He has a good nose for BS."

Jenny flipped through my documents, scanning the temporary restraining order. Looking up, she inquired, "So, what's your story? What do I need to know?"

I had typed, in chronological order, notes of the key elements that Jenny should be aware of. How I met Milos, when I started financially supporting him, when I found out he was married, the dates of the domestic violence, and anything that I knew to be a lie thus far with physical proof.

It took me almost two hours to give her the full recap. By the end, her face was pure astonishment. She didn't speak right away, her brain still processing the pure insanity of my situation.

"He's fucking crazy! He is fucking crazy!" She leaned back in her chair, away from the paper on which she had been scribbling down notes.

I couldn't help but laugh.

Right on the money.

Deciding to go with her as my legal representative, now was the time to actually build the evidence we were going to need. Jenny gave me homework. She needed statements from anyone who had witnessed Milos being violent or aggressive, anyone he had told he was mafia. They would have to type up a short account of when they met Milos, how they knew him, and anything pertinent that the judge would need to know. Based on their statements, Jenny would decide whether or not to call them as potential witnesses.

She also suggested I hire a private investigator. Someone who could look into things internationally. We were hunting for any information about Milos or his family in Serbia, plus letting the PI interview the key players, some being Milos's friends and supposed colleagues.

Jenny tasked the office paralegal to order the documents pertaining to Milos's divorce, as well. I knew his case number, so it would be easy enough to track down. My shiny new lawyer wanted to see if there was anything in the court files that would be helpful in our litigation.

Piece after piece of the puzzle started to unfold.

Remember Bunny? I emailed her. If he lied about cancer, he probably lied about not cheating.

Apologizing, I explained that Milos had told me that she was blackmailing him, but recent events had proved that he couldn't be trusted.

That woman, more than anyone, provided the most eye-opening information.

Here is Bunny's response to my first email:

Hi Brittani,

I'm so sorry that this happened to you and you didn't deserve any of it. During the time I sent you all of those screenshots, I did some further investigation into his past and I knew that he literally had no money and all of his stories were lies. He used to live with an older wealthy lady and her son and tried to tell me it was his "Grandma's House." He never played tennis professionally, he would show another guy's name on stats charts who is 19 years old that also lives in Serbia. A famous pianist from Belgrade who is 55 has the same name and he used to show me compositions, pretending that they were his. He's also not a doctor and was a research assistant at FHH, not even close to becoming a plastic surgeon like he claimed.

Feel free to call me if you need any information and if you need help with anything. I can't imagine how you're feeling right now and I've never met anyone who lied and deceived so much. I would stay away from his "cousin" Lazar who is actually not related to him at all. My number is ###-###-####.

—Bunny

* * * * *

The older wealthy lady had to be Oksana. Lazar wasn't his cousin? Roger that. Bunny was also right about him having no tennis ranking, which I had already deduced. He had told me that he went to a musical academy and wrote ballads, but I had never seen him play any sort of instrument. There was a Milos Mihajlovic who pulled up as a composer when you searched his name online, but it wasn't my Milos.

At least his lies were consistent.

It took a moment for one sentence of her email to really register.

He was not a doctor.

I felt sick. Who was this man that I let into my home, my heart, and my bed?

Milos not being an MD, or working at FHH, made perfect sense. Why was he always studying but never actually passing his board exams? A brilliant ruse: he could easily pose as a European doctor, and if anyone sought his advice or treatment, he wasn't legally allowed to comment until he was board-certified.

There were a few doctors named Milos Mihajlovic who had attended the medical school he claimed to have graduated from in Belgrade. Did Milos go online and decide to create a persona around anyone with his exact moniker? Talk about insanity.

No money? Not that I had ever cared, but that made perfect sense as well.

Zora's suitcase was old and tattered. She had one nice purse, which Oksana probably purchased for her. Not to mention, she hadn't paid for a single thing during our time together. Not, one, penny.

Like mother, like maybe son.

Did she even travel from Serbia for Misha's birth? If you remember, I had never accompanied Milos to pick her up at the airport. She could reside in the United States currently, for all I knew!

"In our culture, if you are a guest, you are not allowed to pay for anything. You will see when you come to Serbia someday, try to take out your wallet around Zora or Nikola, see what happens," Milos had said.

This statement put the expectation onto me that I was to do the same, because she was my guest.

After Bunny, I found the FHH website and an email address for Doctor Lancaster, the head of surgery at the hospital where Milos claimed he had been working. My email to him was a bit more cautious:

Hi Joe,

You never have met me, but when I first started dating Milos, he mentioned you often. I have a 3.5 month old son now with him. He said he worked as a research assistant for you, and had a surgery residency that he ended up turning down because he couldn't finish his boards in time. Wanted to see if you could provide some insight?

Thank you for your time!

—*Brittani*

Six hours later, Joe responded.

Brittani,

Milos and I haven't spoken in over a year. True, he was supposed to work at my lab, but he never spent any time actually in it. Apologies, when it comes to his residency, I have no clue what you are talking about.

That is all the insight I can provide.

—*Joe*

* * * * *

Rushing to Milos's LinkedIn and Facebook pages, I took screenshots where he had listed that he was working at FHH before he had a chance to delete the evidence.

Milos had dropped by the hospital administrative office, had his photo taken and received an ID badge, and then disappeared. All he needed was that badge to prove to me and countless others that he was indeed employed where he said he was employed. A piece of plastic with a photo and a logo was enough for none of us to investigate the matter any further.

All of this new information was overwhelming.

At this point, I did hire a private investigator. One with years of experience who specialized in social media. This was becoming bigger than I could handle on my own. With Jenny's encouragement, we created a list of questions and people for him to contact.

* * * * *

Back to Bunny. We ended up talking on the phone. She had offered her number, and she thought she might have more vital information. It was comforting for me to have someone else who would understand the level of deception I was feeling.

If only I had spoken to Bunny when she first reached out, I would have known that she was telling the truth. She described my mother's house, where Milos had been FaceTiming her while we were visiting. He had told her that I was just a friend who took care of Lui, and that he stayed at my house sometimes when he didn't want to drive back to San Diego.

Bunny wasn't a call girl, but a very successful entrepreneur. She was articulate, funny, and duped. Just like me.

According to my newfound friend, Milos was a good wingman, hanging out with Jurica, Lazar, and Joe—men with money, status, and power. They loved having him around because he was attractive and excellent at picking up women. He boasted at dinners when they were all together about his family's KGB ties and their extensive wealth. The rich boys let Milos into their inner circle because they thought he was one of them.

Bunny also had more information on Oksana. From what Lazar had told her, Milos's wife was a trust fund baby. Millions of dollars and homes in Beverly Hills, Malibu, Hollywood, all over the world.

Before hanging up, she offered to testify at my trial and urged me to call her if I needed anything. I thanked her, the new information about Oksana urging me to dig deeper.

Finding his wife's Instagram, I discovered that she was not a grandma as Milos had described, but she was Russian and gorgeous. Long, straight black hair with bangs and blue eyes, Oksana looked like an older version of Milla Jovovich with lip injections. I only hope when I am in my forties that I look that hot, minus the filler.

All the photos of Milos had obviously been removed, but I gasped when I spotted a picture on her profile of her with Lui as a puppy. Finding her Facebook, I saw that Anto had also taken photos of her, and her teenage son had even more snapshots with Lui.

Oksana had more than likely purchased Lui for Milos.

Suddenly, I realized why Zora and Nikola were so upset when he started dating me. The fighting, the tension. Now, I highly doubted that he'd had a plane ticket back to Serbia when we met and had given up running the "family businesses" to be together. Zora and Nikola were livid because he had left his extremely wealthy wife before they had a chance to squeeze any real money out of her.

Milos used to say all the time, "I had everything when I met you. I had everything."

He really did. No more lavish vacations and private jets. He was a kept man and he threw it all away because he found me fascinating. Probably the challenge of my initial resistance turned him on and made him want me more. Or he was sick of sleeping with someone almost twice his age.

Another tidbit from Bunny:

Milos was forced to return his black Lexus, the car he had when we first met, because Oksana was paying for it. Not because it was "time to turn it back in" as he had led me to believe.

A text message from Lazar to Bunny dated March 10, 2017:

"Milos was just here for lunch. He has been asking about you."

Now I knew where some of the car miles had come from, as he had been driving to LA and back to hang out with Lazar. Bunny again, a wealth of information:

"You know his supposed Aunt Mary in San Diego? According to Lazar, it isn't really his aunt! She was his host-mom when he was an exchange student in Idaho back when he was in high school. He wasn't on a tennis scholarship," she also divulged.

The whether or not he was a doctor part was highly confusing. I had personally witnessed him studying medical books for hours on end and finishing over eight thousand questions in practice exams. But he didn't know his glove size at Misha's birth. He didn't know where his spleen was on his stomach, and he had been in the United States for over three years without passing the board exams needed to practice medicine in the state of California.

Scary thought—was Milos trying to game the system? Faked his diploma and grades, and attempted to pass the medical boards without having ever attended medical school at all?

Or did he even take any of the tests?

Was his name even Milos?

The first time he had chased and grabbed me, in my old house with Misha still in my stomach, I could have sworn I hadn't touched his right cornea. He knew me too well and he knew that I would feel guilty if I thought I had harmed him. Now, I believed it was another lie. Milos's eye didn't have a single mark; it wasn't red or swollen anywhere. Again, he didn't let me go to the doctor with him.

He just needed a quick excuse to level the playing field.

I should have left him the first time he had physically attacked me.

The private investigator, under my lawyer's instruction, had contacted Doctor Bernard, the individual that Milos claimed let him assist in his plastic surgery practice.

While Doctor Bernard did know of him, they had hung out a few times, he had never let Milos assist in any surgeries, only allowing him to observe one facelift. The photo on Zora's social media page with Milos in scrubs, cap, and face mask from Doctor Bernard's practice? Just that, a photo of him in scrubs, not actually doing anything.

There weren't any pictures of Milos in medical school anywhere online that I could find, nor had I ever been shown any. How had I not realized this before? He said that he had graduated early, and Zora had gone and picked up his diploma in his place. Medical school is many years of commitment, right? Suspicious, as there should have been at least one photo of him in the lab, or in scrubs with his classmates, or of Zora accepting his diploma for him.

You're probably saying to yourself, "I would have been onto him way sooner! Girl, what took you so long?"

If I had discovered any of the findings above on my own and questioned him myself, he would have had an immediate and convincing answer erasing any doubt.

There was always a lie that was believable to cover up the truth.

Thank the Lord I didn't give him my bank account information to help Zora "transfer funds" from Serbia for his "cancer." They would have probably wiped me clean.

More and more and more falsehoods were uncovered.

The coffee company he said his family owned? Lie.

The property in Montenegro that was unfinished, which he was trying to get Maya, my real estate friend, to sell? Lie.

The water company he had showed me, and also offered to Maya to market? Lie.

The furniture company? It was a real company, but again, they were not the owners.

You can come up with your own conclusions, but here is what I thought was going on.

Milos and his family were leeches. Pretending to own certain enterprises or brands in the hopes they could strike sales or deals that would earn them commissions. By hanging out with wealthy entrepreneurs, they would try to figure out how to broker partnerships that would siphon some dough their direction.

The scary question looming in the back of my mind was, "Are they really underworld players? Are they running or involved in any sort of mafia organization?"

That was hard to prove.

I still don't know. My gut said yes. Yes, they are dangerous, yes, they are treacherous, yes, they are deceitful, yes, they are ruthless, and yes, they will do and say anything to get what they want.

I had to win this court battle. I had to get full custody of Misha, and I had to keep him from their grasp.

Jenny received back the packet from the LA court pertaining to his divorce. Oksana was the petitioner, meaning that she was the one filing for divorce. Milos had already been hitched, back in 2015, to Oksana. Which meant he was married and living with her when he started dating me.

Busy guy, no wonder he was always tired!

It was urgent that we talk to Oksana. She had to have information that would be extremely pertinent to my pending trial. The private investigator found a phone number for her and was able to speak with her briefly. Disappointing, as she refused to comment or answer any of our probing questions. The only thing she did say was, "I thought that he loved me."

Filthy. Used. Dirty. Disgusting. It is so hard to explain how I felt during all of this, besides rushing to my ob-gyn to get tested for every STD currently known to man. Luckily, all came back clean, which was a miracle.

If Milos wasn't using a condom with me, you can bet your buttons he wasn't using one with anyone else.

All of the older ladies he taught tennis? He was probably sleeping with them, too.

Even his "Aunt Mary" acted like a jealous girlfriend the one and only time that we had had dinner together.

My first trial date loomed closer and closer as I spent hour after hour, day after day, racking my brain over anything he had said, anyone Milos had mentioned, anything that could be profound and impactful.

In all of this, I also started to take precautions in protecting myself. Reporting the copy of my birth certificate stolen to the state agency in Minnesota. An alert was submitted to the passport office, so that if anyone tried to apply for a passport for Misha, I would be notified.

My credit was frozen, so Milos or whoever wouldn't be able to open any accounts in my name and with my social security number.

I also started to reconnect with the friends I had neglected, filling them in on the shit show that had become my life. It was a good gal pal of mine, Lisa, who explained to me what a sociopath was.

Someone who lies, is charismatic, and lacks any emotional empathy. They control and isolate their victims. They only feel anger. They smile when they think they have power over someone, enjoying the manipulation.

The most dangerous wing in any hospital is where they house the sociopaths. Many lawyers, politicians, CEOs of companies, people in positions with clout and notoriety, were sociopaths. They literally didn't care who they hurt or what they had to do to get to where they wanted to go.

"You have to read the *Sociopath Next Door*! My brother was dating a sociopath! Trust me, Milos is one too!" Lisa told me on one of our many calls. She kept checking in, a mom herself, worried sick.

Of course, I ordered the book and only managed to get twenty or so pages in before putting it down.

Milos was, and is, a sociopath.

Chapter 16

TRIAL AND ERROR

April 17, 2017

"Brittani, we are going to trial. This hearing is preliminary. We will explain to the judge that we have witnesses and evidence to present and we will need more than the allotted time. Trust me."

Jenny had told me such, but I was still a terrified wreck as I sat inside the courthouse, alone.

I wasn't ready to see Milos again. I wasn't going to look at him, and I wasn't going to glance up when I heard his voice.

If I did look into his eyes, I might back down, and I couldn't afford to lose.

Ding, a text from Jenny.

"Just sit next to courtroom A, at the door. I will meet you there."

As I was reading her message, I did indeed hear my tormenter entering the crowded lobby. The table where I was waiting was at the very front, next to the Sheriff's station where every person coming in had to go through a metal detector.

"Good morning Bill, how are you?"

It's him. Clenching my hands together to keep them from shaking any harder, I kept my head down. Think of Misha. Think of your son. Be strong.

A shadow of a man stepped to the side of the table, forcing me to look up.

Bill Hurman, Milos's lawyer. He was tall, probably pretty close to Milos's height. In his early forties with shockingly white hair that was expertly styled. His suit was pinstripe and tailored, classy, with an "I'm important" and "you can trust me" vibe. If I had thought Lazar was shady, he was nothing compared to this guy.

Talking down to me, he arranged his features into concern.

"You are Brittani, right? Is your lawyer present?"

Come on, Jenny! Get here already! I couldn't stand to be alone in this building for one more second!

"She will be here any moment," I replied, trying to make it clear that I didn't want to talk.

"Good, good. Well, when you see her, I would like to have a word with her before we start. Just point me out and send her my way." He smiled and turned. I didn't dare look back to see where he had stashed Milos during our interlude.

Finally, Jenny came rushing in. She was always in a hurry—I wasn't her only client. You could tell that her brain never turned off, and she squeezed every second out of every day to the max potential.

"Hey Brittani! How are you holding up?" She sat down opposite me, happily depositing her heavy binder and briefcase on the table between us.

"Milos's lawyer is looking for you, Bill something?"

I didn't even have to point him out before he was back next to the desk, making his introductions.

Jenny was polite, licking her fingers and flipping through her binder, pulling out paperwork that needed to be filed before we went before the judge.

"Do you have a moment to talk? I really need you to see something before we proceed," Milos's lawyer was asking Jenny.

She was getting irritated, as she had budgeted her time and hadn't expected this rendezvous.

"I have to go file these right now, but maybe in a bit?" Jenny answered, then turned to me. "You going be okay here alone?"

I nodded my head, afraid that if I spoke, it would be stuttered gibberish.

Not exactly a brush-off, she wasn't rude, but it was clear that she wasn't going to follow his lead as she walked away. Bill chased after her. Another good twenty minutes went by before a harassed Jenny returned. She once again sat down and leaned forward, not wanting our conversation to be overhead.

"That guy followed me downstairs! He is saying that they have a recording. 'If we listen to this, we are going to drop the restraining order,' and he kept insisting that whatever is on it will nullify your claims. In all my years of practicing law, I have never had another lawyer follow me like that."

Jenny held up a small thumb drive.

Instantly, I started to panic.

What was on it? He was recording me? What did he record?

I didn't even notice the bailiff calling our names to enter, or changing rooms, or Judge Linden agreeing that our case was going to trial. All I could think about was that darn thumb drive, and not looking at Milos.

I should have been relieved, as the judge agreed to let Misha and I leave the state to "visit" my mom in Arizona. As long as the court was made aware of our address. He knew what Jenny was really asking, to let us exit for safety reasons, but Jenny put it in a way that made it easy for him to say yes.

Eventually, I was outside the courthouse with a worried Jenny as we walked back to her car. She insisted on giving me a ride to my mode of transportation, afraid of me walking alone with Milos in close proximity.

"Do you want to come back to my office and listen to this together?" she asked, indicating the thumb drive.

Only when we were at her desk, with the door closed, did she dare put the tiny device into her computer and open the audio files. There were two. Part of me wanted her to eject the thing and let me smash it with a hammer, concerned that Milos had put some sort of spyware or something of that nature.

Hesitating, Jenny clicked on the first file labeled: 12/15/2016. The moment it started playing, I heard the running water of the shower.

That fucking low-life asshole had recorded me, while I was heartbroken, naked, showering, nine days after giving birth, and only four days after kicking Zora and him out.

That was why he was smiling. Goading me on, because this was his insurance policy. He had a card to play if I ever stepped out of line. Milos, and his lawyer, who happened to be a criminal lawyer. Odd, because this was a family matter. Either way, they were trying to blackmail me.

Listening to myself cry and break, thinking I was having a personal moment now with Jenny as a witness, wasn't uncomfortable. It was empowering. Instead of the fear that was my constant companion these days, I was angry. How dare he!

Milos let himself in that night, he pushed my buttons and mocked my grief, on purpose.

The hardest parts to listen to were myself saying, "I want to die."

I didn't mean that I actually wanted to die, I meant that I was in so much turmoil that it was almost too much to stand. You try giving birth and going through a breakup in the same week! A therapist since has told me it is something called transference. Trying to express the pain I was feeling inside, but not actually wanting to cause physical harm. Duh.

Jenny paused the twenty-minute recording after roughly ten, not wanting to have to bill me to listen to the entire thing.

"Let's see really quickly what is on the second recording, and then talk."

Labeled "Pediatrician," she hit play.

Milos had also been recording me again the day he had moved back in. The day of the second domestic violence incident when I had been huddled on the carpet after he took my phone, hurt me, and was holding Misha. Changing tactics, stating that I had postpartum to get him to calm down and hand my son back to my safe arms.

Jenny hit pause and looked at me.

"What do you want to do? He can leak these. He can put them online, and we wouldn't have a hard time proving that he was the culprit, but the damage would already be done."

Gathering my thoughts, I was furious. Milos had to be stopped.

"There are a lot of good things on those recordings too. I talk about the verbal abuse, and his awful mother, his control and manipulation of me. Granted, the whole part about 'wanting to die' might not look the best, but I still think I have a strong case. If he leaks them, he leaks them. I am not backing down. I say, we go forward."

Jenny sighed, but she liked my answer.

"Okay."

Chapter 17

WAITING AND WORRYING

It is illegal in the state of California to record someone without their permission, did you know that? Penal Code 632. Two-party state, which means both parties must be aware that they are being recorded. That didn't mean Bill wouldn't try to use it to impeach me. Not that I planned on lying about anything under oath.

I could probably write another memoir just on the trial alone. It was long, and brutal, but let's just stick to the highlights.

May 22, 2017

Day one. Surprise! Milos had enlisted in the army. The very same day I had left for Los Angeles in March. He must have known he wasn't getting another green card through marrying me, as his first one through Oksana was set to expire in August. According to Bill, we had to finish the trial before he started basic training, as he was having the great honor of being enlisted as the first Serbian doctor in the United States Armed Forces.

Confusing, as I was pretty sure he wasn't a doctor.

More on his army shenanigans later, might as well get into the actual proceedings.

As the petitioner, my side was given the opportunity to go first. And the first person on the stand was of course, me. Jenny walked me through, establishing the foundation of our relationship, and specific instances of Milos lashing out. She had me fully recount the first and second time he had hurt me physically, and other instances of his erratic behavior.

I wished the appointed magistrate could have looked into my mind, because Milos had left it scarred, bloody, and bruised.

"Miss Taylor, I need you to speak slower. See the court reporter? She can't follow what you are saying if you don't talk slower," the judge barked at me. Repeatedly.

Great, I didn't think he liked me. Judge Linden was crabby and overworked, in his sixties, if I had to guess. A full head of pepper hair with thick glasses perched on the end of his nose. Even with his bifocals, you could see that his eyes were shrewd. The honorable judge Harry Linden didn't miss a thing.

June 12, 2017

Trial day two.

This time, a man named Robert Pond went first. He had started out working on my mom's property in Arizona, helping to take care of her horses, but he had quickly become family.

Robert was like my brother and a given at every special event and holiday. He had also developed a friendship with Milos during the course of our courtship. They talked on the phone and texted often, sometimes daily.

Honest and straightforward, Robert was extremely likable. He reminded the court how I had called him after Milos had barred the door and wouldn't let me leave, the same afternoon I had confronted Milos about his porn habit. One of the many occasions of abuse that I had forgotten about.

There were just too many traumatic moments to keep track.

Robert was valuable to my case because he had been my confidant when I couldn't go to my mother, in fear that she would hate Milos for his treatment of her only daughter.

Milos had also told Robert that he had cancer, and that he and his family had ties to the mafia and Russian mobsters, all which Robert testified to under oath.

I am not even going to bother going into Bill's cross-examination. He was purposely unprepared, shuffling papers, pauses after each question, running the clock down.

After Robert came my mother.

By far, one of the hardest things to watch was my poor maternal figure on the stand.

Wanting to make the most of time we had left, Jenny quickly laid the foundation of how Barbara knew Milos and then jumped straight into the specific instances of his rages, what she had observed.

I was the crier in the family, my mother always the pillar of strength. It was excruciating to watch her face crumble, grief that she had hidden from me pouring out as she whispered into the microphone on the stand.

Jenny brought up the night in December when Milos went to strike her for coming into the room with Misha in pursuit of diapers and baby wipes.

Her sorrow was palpable. So thick in the air that everyone, even the bailiff, was affected.

"He almost kind of throws the baby wipes and diapers to me, and I left. And I left Brittani, you know? I went back and I took care of the baby, but I left Brittani. I left her there, screaming. She's in a ball, and she is crying hysterically, and I left. I left. Why did I leave? I should have called the police. I should have done something. I didn't. I didn't do anything," she testified.

My mom blamed herself.

The truth was, she was scared of Milos, too.

July 24, 2017

Trial day three.

We were forced to subpoena Officer Miller, the police officer who took down the domestic violence report, as Bill wasn't going to let in the report if he wouldn't testify.

Sleazy Bill appeared to be using every underhanded tactic in the book. Pretending that he didn't receive documents even with an email confirmation from Jenny's firm that he had, continually unprepared, slower than a slug when he had the floor, no questions ready, and making things up on the fly.

Jenny, on the other hand, was a warrior. She knew the dates and events of my case inside out and was beyond prepared, even with her rebuttals to any potential objections that Bill might throw out there for certain items being entered into evidence. I had a champagne lawyer on a beer budget, and she couldn't have been more tenacious.

When Officer Miller was up on the stand, I started to have the feeling that we were winning.

Judge Linden tipped me off when he didn't wait for Jenny to ask a question, but asked it himself.

The officer had just described how I had waited two months to report the incident, but he believed I had done so because Milos had told me that "he had gotten his master's in forensic pathology because he wanted to learn how to kill people and get away with it."

The judge then leaned over and asked the witness directly, "Did you make any observations or anything about her credibility at the time when she told you that?"

Officer Miller was earnest in his response. "It did not seem like she was lying to me. Based on my interactions with many, many other domestic violence victims."

The elderly judge leaned back, nodding his head as if to say "yup, that is what I thought."

After the police officer came Bunny's testimony.

She had ignored subpoenas to the previous two court dates, with good reason.

Milos's friends had been calling her and sending threatening texts. I also had received blocked calls on the regular, I just never answered them.

Meeting Bunny for the first time, I saw why Milos had liked her. She was not only gorgeous, with a thick mane of stick straight natural red hair, but she was quick-witted and bold. Proving so as she walked straight up to the witness box, in a daring dress and stilettos, looked over at where Milos was sitting, and flashed her pearly whites.

I didn't dare look at Milos for his reaction, but Bunny was a force of nature.

No wonder Milos and his cronies had tried desperately to keep her out of this.

Bunny rattled off dates and facts, smoothly and with style. Milos had told her as well that his family was connected to the KGB, but she also testified that she didn't believe him. Bunny wasn't scared of Milos, because it was obvious that she would have never tolerated his tantrums for a second.

She wore the pants in any relationship, period.

The clincher was the end of Jenny's direct examination of Bunny.

Jenny stated to the judge that she had just one more inquiry, after revealing that Bunny had been receiving threatening phone calls. The witness wasn't willing to discuss what was said in the calls, and Judge Linden wasn't going to force her.

"I don't want to put her in what she believes to be an uncomfortable or dangerous position."

Good, the judge understood the severity of the situation. Jenny couldn't have picked a better question to finish with.

"Just one more, your honor," Jenny said. "Bunny, the threats that you received, I just want to clarify, were they in relation to your testimony today?"

Bunny was miffed, but answered anyways.

"Yes," she admitted.

Slam dunk.

At the end of her testimony, I was back up on the stand.

Milos had hit his head against the shelf above my crib, back on January 21, 2017.

Bill and his client were trying now to spin that I had pushed him into the shelf, which was crazy, as I wasn't even in the townhouse at the time and Barbara was holding Misha on our bed, witnessing the entire debacle.

My mother swore that he threw himself against the shelf on purpose, forgetting that she was also in the room.

We were prepared for this one. I had a YouTube video in which I was sitting in Milos's lap and he talked about hitting his head. In it, I was teasing him for his clumsiness. When I played it on my laptop for the court, it was pretty clear that I didn't do it. Bill quickly dropped his line of questioning, knowing that another one of Milos's lies wasn't going to stick.

He switched gears again, trying to enter into evidence the illegal recordings he had also tried to blackmail us with months prior.

Jenny thought the best defense was offense. We had already talked about the contents of the recordings, in detail, so there was nothing on them that could possibly be used for impeachment purposes. It didn't mean sticky Bill wasn't going to try, but Linden shut him down quickly.

"You can't use it. If she didn't agree to it, without her permission, it's inadmissible, period," the judge stated. He shook his head, scolding Bill like he was a little boy who needed a talking to.

"How do you get past the fact that it's illegal that he recorded her? How do you get past that?"

July 31, 2017

Trial day four.

It was apparent that Bill was trying to draw this out. I had found a Yelp review, good 'ole Yelp, in which a client of his had thanked him for using "unique tactics" to stretch out a case for so long that it was eventually deemed a mistrial and thrown out. I printed the review, brought it with me to court, and showed it to Jenny, who gasped.

"Oh my God, you're right!" she exclaimed. "If he keeps stalling like he's been doing, I am going to show this to the judge."

Jenny and I were onto Bill. He knew how pricey it was to go to trial, and that most people could not afford a long, drawn out affair. He was trying to outspend me, and make it until mid-August, at which point Milos would be in basic training and unavailable for six months.

The three hours in court went painfully slow, filled with Bill's intentional incompetence as Milos was now finally on the stand.

Where Bill hadn't objected much when Jenny had the floor, Jenny was all over Bill like a fly on bread. She didn't give him an inch as he questioned Milos, interrupting his flow with a brutal accuracy.

Not once did I look up. I kept my eyes on the table.

We returned two days later.

August 2, 2017

Barbara, Misha, and I had driven through the night to make it into San Diego the following morning. Milos had coaxed a letter from his army recruiter stating that he would be "unavailable" for our, hopefully, final court date and Judge Linden wasn't going to have it.

He wasn't going to let Milos and Bill get away that easily, clearing his schedule so Bill and Milos would have no excuse as to why they couldn't return and finish.

Finally, it was time for Jenny's cross-examination of Milos.

Jenny. Was. A. Beast.

She controlled the narrative, requesting Judge Linden to instruct Milos to give only yes or no answers to certain queries.

My favorite part was when she got to the line of questioning about his "illness." Jenny nailed him to the wall.

"You also told Brittani that you had cancer, correct?"

Milos's face was mournful, trying to look meek and innocent.

"I said that they're suspecting me to have cancer, yes."

Jenny: "Who is 'they'?"

Milos: "Doctors."

Jenny: "Which doctors?"

Milos: "Oncologists."

Jenny: "What is the name of your oncologist that suspected that you had cancer?"

Milos paused, went to speak, paused again. He was caught in a lie and scrambling. I wanted to laugh, it was so comical to me. His mouth opened and closed like a mackerel.

Jenny was the fisherman, and Milos had just fallen for her bait.

"I can take a look at my medical records and tell you?" he mumbled.

Please. You have "cancer" and you don't know the name of the MD that diagnosed you? He couldn't just make up a doctor on the spot or list someone he already knew, because I had my laptop open during his testimony and was ready to fact check if needed.

Jenny smiled, knowing that she had just shown Judge Linden that Milos was lying under oath.

"If it would refresh your recollection, go ahead," she said, pushing him further.

His face was now red with embarrassment.

"I don't have them with me."

Changing directions, Jenny probed further. "Where does your oncologist work?"

"UCLA."

That was news to me. Milos claimed during our relationship that he was being treated at a hospital close to our townhouse in San Diego. It was obvious why he threw this tidbit in, hoping to complicate any further investigation into his claims.

It was also becoming obvious that, yet again, we weren't going to finish. What was supposed to be a two-day trial had turned into five days over five months.

Five months of having to be silent, waiting and worrying. Wondering if Judge Linden was going to rule in my favor.

Even with the ticking clock, Jenny decided to put me back up on the stand, for the very last time. Bill had called me up to that box every single trial date for his "cross examination," which he refused to rest on. He had attacked me from every angle for hours on end. The more he tried to make me look bad, the more it worked in my favor because I had more time to talk. Turning his questions around on him, using them to discuss Milos's duplicity in greater detail.

Back in that box, for the very last time, so physically and mentally drained by the process, I was ready for everything to finally be over.

"Brittani, can I ask you, why do you need this restraining order?" Jenny asked, gently.

My lawyer was a ball of nerves herself. She had fought for me, and you could tell she wondered if it had been enough.

This time, I did look at Milos. I looked at the man that had ruined me.

I looked him in the eyes as I said, "I don't want him to be able to hurt me anymore. I don't want him to be able to hurt my son. I don't want him to be able to hurt my mom. I don't want him to be able to be near me or talk to me. I want him out of my life."

His expression was blank.

Judge Linden asked us if we were willing to come back that afternoon so we could actually finish. After any closing statements, he would be ready to rule.

That smart judge had Bill and Milos over a barrel. They had no valid excuses why they couldn't return, and Jenny and I heartily accepted his offer.

We were given an hour recess, in which Jenny desperately wanted a coffee, so we walked to a little market across from the brick building of the court house.

"Did you see him when I got to his cancer?" Jenny asked. "He was lying! That little shit was lying! I just wanted to reach over and strangle him!" Her hands were up, ready to throttle the invisible respondent in front of her.

I busted out laughing.

The tension had just been too much, and it felt good to let off a little steam.

Jenny bought me a banana and a protein bar, but my stomach was in knots. We headed back to the courthouse and sat once again at the table closest to the door. My feisty lawyer snuck off with her binder, wanting to prepare her closing argument.

It was odd. Milos hadn't called a single witness during the entire proceeding. Not his supposed aunt, Zora, Jurica, Lazar, or any of his influential friends. He should have brought them in as character witnesses, or to try and paint a pretty picture of the man he pretended to be. But here is the rub. If he had brought them into court, they might have learned some of his dirty little secrets, and he couldn't risk it.

Sure, Jurica, Zora, and another guy he played tennis with, wrote character letters—but the judge wouldn't accept them into evidence. They needed to testify to the contents of their statements, as a letter could be easily manipulated.

Trying to keep my mind busy, I just sat there and prayed. I prayed to God that all of this had been worth it.

Jenny gave an Oscar worthy closing statement, full of passion and conviction. Bill's was unorganized and short, more spewing about how Milos was a doctor and joining the army and that I just wanted to punish him for leaving.

Spending a small fortune on lawyer fees just to punish someone? Please.

No sooner was Bill done with his closing speech than Judge Linden was ready to rule.

"In a domestic violence restraining order, as Miss Phillips has stated, the burden of proof here is by a preponderance of the evidence. That means it's more likely than not that domestic violence has been committed," the judge announced.

Jenny grabbed my hand as I choked up, happy tears for once streaming down my cheeks.

"When I look at the credibility of the parties, starting with Brittani, I did find her credible for the most part. I found her confused, but credible. I think that everything she told me, she believed. She was credible about the events. She was credible about her fear of the respondent. You argue that it wasn't rational. I found her to be credible in that sense. I found her credible regarding the incidents surrounding the DV and control issues. I did find that her fear is reasonable."

On August 2, 2017, I was awarded a two-year permanent restraining order against Milos. He was not to try to contact me, come within one hundred yards, or harass me in any way, shape, or form. He was also not allowed to handle a firearm or ammunition while the restraining order was in effect.

To give you some context, most restraining orders are six months to a year. Two years was severe and assuring. Judge Linden continued with his findings.

"Do I think he is mafia or KGB? No. Do I think he is a doctor? I don't know," he continued. "I think he went to medical school. He keeps calling himself a doctor. I think that is a technicality."

In over fifteen hours of trial, even Milos and his lawyer were not able to prove that he was indeed a Doctor of Medicine. No physical evidence was presented, besides the Xeroxed copies of his supposed transcripts and medical diploma.

Whether or not Milos and his family are indeed involved in organized crime is still a mystery. Sure, Judge Linden disagreed, but he also didn't live with Milos for over a year. I was the one who witnessed the calls and emails back and forth between Nikola and my former lover.

Would they really stage something daily toward their "business" to keep up an act? Photoshop documents constantly, email them to each other, and then have Milos talk audibly about the supposed deals so I could overhear?

What would be the point of the ruse? I was not rich, not like Oksana.

Still so many unanswered questions.

In the judge's eyes, we weren't able to prove it, besides the verbal confirmation of multiple witnesses who Milos had told that he and his family have mob ties. How about this. Maybe they are that good at hiding any sort of paper trail. Or, even scarier, Milos was trying to manifest his lies due to his sociopathic nature?

Either way, good riddance.

The restraining order was going to put a damper on Milos's military career, at least as long as it was in effect. If he couldn't handle a firearm, he couldn't complete basic training.

"He is going into the army, your honor," Bill whined, irritated that his games and tactics didn't pan out.

"He is an army doctor. He has to ask for an exception if he somehow needs a weapon for that. I am not saying it is right. I am just saying he is not the first person going into the military that has a restraining order. He will have to work that out with the military," the judge said firmly. It was clear that his decision was final.

I thanked Jenny a million times, as she had been vital in our win, and headed back to the hotel.

Hugging my son to my chest, the first time in a very long time, I relaxed.

Chapter 18

REX

Not wanting to confuse you guys, but I haven't called Misha his given name since Milos moved out for good.

Lemme explain, 'k?

Milos was a controlling monster. What he said, went, or there were repercussions. He said our son was going to have a Serbian name, and that was that.

I never got to do the normal mom or parent thing. You know, where you pick out a name, or maybe ten, and roll them around on your tongue until one really speaks to you. Not to mention that I didn't know if his grandfather Misha was even a real person or had ever really existed.

Very little of what Milos had told me turned out to be actually true. This is an understatement.

Laugh out loud.

My mom and I tried out Oliver for a week. A name I had always liked, but my son just didn't respond to it. And the more

I called him "Oliver," the more I didn't like it, either—too many syllables.

Deciding to research old Hollywood actors' names, I stumbled upon Rex.

Rex.

It was short, manly, and my little Rex already screeched like a baby dinosaur when he was excited.

"What about Rex?" I ask my mom, who was playing with my precious angel on the couch.

His little baby cheeks stretched into a smile. And they did every time I said his new name.

"Rex, Rex, I think he likes it, Rex." I cooed, trying it out.

Hovering above him to observe his reactions, it was clear that the little man approved.

He was now Rex—all I had left to do was make it official on paper. Would he have had an identity crisis every time there was roll call at school? I didn't want to take that chance. There is already so much that I will have to explain when he is old enough, and ready.

This meant two more trial dates, trepidation, and additional expenses. Luckily, yet another judge ruled in our favor, believing, like I did, that it was in the best interest of my child.

Rex Robert Taylor.

Has a nice ring to it, don't you think?

The request for the name change was warranted. It was for his protection, as well. Every police officer and investigator that I have spoken to since leaving Milos have all stated the same: "Do not let your son out of your sight. Do not get him a passport. Do not travel out of the country. If your son is taken, the only way to get him back from Serbia would be hired mercenaries."

Not once during our trial did Milos or his lawyer ask how Rex was doing or try to arrange any sort of visitation, which was good when it came to settling the matter of custody. You think it would have been a done deal, but the restraining order only extended to my son until the new orders were in place.

Judge Linden really must have disliked Milos, as I was awarded full custody. Milos was required to enlist in a fifty-two-week course on domestic violence and a ten-week course in basic parenting skills. He also had to travel to my county of residency if he wanted to see Rex—and the visits had to be supervised by a government agency—for less than two hours at a time, with a maximum of two times a week. Lastly, he had to bear all responsibility for costs pertaining to these visits.

With this arrangement, I was also allowed to move whenever I wanted within the United States, without having to notify Rex's father.

For liberal California courts, these orders were pretty extreme.

You're probably curious if Milos has had any contact with or has tried to see Rex since I left him. And the answer is no. More than likely, he is already on to his next mark, whoever the poor girl, or girls, might be.

Milos was so skilled in his deception. Sometimes I wonder how many other women he has done this to. Does Rex have any half-siblings? How will I explain all of this to him when he is older?

Ask me again in ten years. I am sure that more of my questions will be answered in time.

Back in my childhood home, with my mother and my son, the real healing started. For months after the trial, I wouldn't talk to anyone. Keeping my head down, hamming it up for videos, but the moment I stopped recording, I pulled back into my shell.

I had to grieve. You have to understand that I was totally and completely taken by someone who I had trusted and loved. The happy, loud, confident person I had been was missing and it took a while to find her again. Life in general wasn't bad, he was bad. Yes, I was hurting, but I knew the hurt wouldn't last forever.

Milos wanted to destroy me, and the best revenge would be not to let him.

Fight, bounce back, work hard, take control of my life, and become a dazzling success—that was my new plan.

Surprisingly, this memoir wasn't hard to write. All I needed was a laptop and my memories. Finally getting to tell my truth, and the truth about what really occurred, in my own words, was actually therapeutic.

Part of my pain has been the silence. I have had to be mute and let the internet guess about what happened to me. Writing on gossip forums and making hurtful videos with their conjectures, having no clue about the depth of my pain and struggles. Getting this on paper has been liberating.

I am just lucky that I survived, when so many others in abusive situations often don't. If this is you, reading this right now, get out. Get help. Tell everyone around you. There is strength in numbers, and power in the truth. Continued physical or verbal abuse is never valid or warranted. It is not okay, period.

The hardest step is the first.

I would have gone through everything, all over again, if it meant having my beautiful son. Who, thankfully, isn't a sociopath. He was only five months old and in his walker when I started coughing and choking on some water. As fast as his little legs could propel him, he was next to my chair with his hand on my thigh, looking up at me with eyes full of concern.

He is the sweetest, smartest, funniest, most special little boy, and the reason that I was strong enough to stand up to Milos when so many others hadn't.

All in all, Milos took me for well over a hundred thousand dollars. He took my first home, he took my career, he took away my friends, and he tarnished my self-esteem. But maybe I was supposed to repeat this narrative.

I have a request for you, the reader. Please share my tale, tell your friends, tell anyone who will listen. I want to be a cautionary tale: a sucky love story.

Learn from my mistakes, and don't be afraid to make your own. I still believe in true love, in finding someone who is the omelet to my cheese, but I am in no rush. Being single has been peaceful and safe. My son is thriving, and that is all that matters.

I would say that I am 90 percent back to normal, but part of me will never trust again.

After my trial, I wasn't done digging and, through my exploration into military proceedings, discovered something else. If Milos did indeed enlist as a "doctor" as he had said, he would have gone straight to officer training, not basic training. This much is easily searchable.

Per a FOIA (Freedom of Information Act) request, I also discovered what Milos *actually* enlisted as in the army. Due to government rules, I am not allowed to say more. But his job is the farthest and most mundane thing from a doctor possible. You're just going to have to use your imagination on this one.

I never did find out if Milos really is a doctor, or if he really is in the mafia, but as long as Rex is safe and happy, I'm happy. Do I have security cameras installed now? Absolutely. Am I cautious when we are out in public? Won't let him out of my sight.

Love can break you, but it can also heal. Don't let life's bitter moments turn you sour. Make the biggest glass of lemonade, drink up, and keep going.

Don't be afraid of love. Just do a background check first.

ABOUT THE AUTHOR

Brittani Louise Taylor is an actress, artist, influencer, and the nerdiest cool person you will ever meet. On Youtube alone, her videos have been viewed over 250 million times. She grew up with her nose in a book, and little did she know that someday she would be writing one of her very own. Or that it would be so dramatic, a true story, and pretty dang good, if you ask her. Brittani also has a weakness for organic food, cycling, kittens, and she secretly dreams of one day becoming a contestant on *The Bachelor*. She also dabbles in sarcasm, is a kick-butt mother, and currently resides in Arizona surrounded by cactus.